INSIGHT COMPACT GUIDES

GREAT LITTLE GUIDES

Compact Guide: Portugal is the ultimate quick-reference guide to this land on the edge of Europe. It tells you everything you need to know about the country's attractions, from its stunningly beautiful mountains and coastline to towns and cities shaped by an exciting history of sea-faring and discovery.

This is just one title in *Apa Publications'* new series of pocket-sized, easy-to-use guidebooks intended for the independent-minded traveller. Based on an award-winning formula pioneered in Germany, *Compact Guides* pride themselves on being up-to-date and authoritative. They are in essence mini travel encyclopedias, designed to be comprehensive yet portable, both readable and reliable.

Star Attractions

An instant reference to some of Portugal's most popular tourist attractions to help you on your way.

Lisbon tram p27

Mosteiro dos Jerónimos, Lisbon p27

Oporto p63

Óbidos p36

Batalha Abbey p39

Alentejo p41

Serra da Arrabida p42

Ponte da Piedade p44

Albufeira p46

Folk dancer p92

Buçaco Forest p59

PORTUGAL

Introduction

Portugal – A Land of Diversity 5
Historical Highlights 10

Places

Route 1: Lisbon – The White City 14
Route 2: Costa do Sol – Serra de Sintra – Mafra 30
Route 3: Óbidos – Alcobaça – Batalha – Fátima – Tomar 36
Route 4: Alentejo and the Algarve 41
Route 5: Alto Alentejo and the Ribatejo 50
Route 6: Coimbra 52
Route 7: Aveiro – Buçaco – Dão 58
Route 8: Oporto 63
Route 9: The Minho: Guimarães – Braga 71
Route10: The Douro and Trás-os-Montes 78

Culture

Art History 83

Leisure

Food and Drink 89
Nightlife 92
Shopping 93

Practical Information

Getting There 95
Getting Around 96
Facts for the Visitor 97
Accommodation 100

Index 104

Portugal – A Land of Diversity

Opposite: a piece of the Algarve

More than 500 years have elapsed since Portuguese seafarers set out to discover unknown continents and bring back untold wealth which once made Portugal the richest country on earth. The glorious events of the past still live on in the national consciousness. Built in 1960, the Discoveries Monument in the Lisbon suburb of Belém, points straight out into the broad Atlantic, wistfully gazing back on that Golden Age. The legacies of those days, and the epochs that went before and after, remain as a lasting reminder of a rich and eventful past. Magnificent buildings and other works of art dot the landscape. Churches, monasteries and palaces are decorated with exquisite, distinctly Portuguese features, such as *azulejo* tiles and Manueline sculptures, often reflecting the country's maritime heritage.

But works of art and architecture are not the only attraction that this country on the edge of Europe has to offer. Travellers arriving by car from Spain will be struck by the difference between the arid, treeless expanses they have left behind, and the compact, verdant landscape that lies ahead. Passing through rolling hills and mountains, across broad plains patched with cork oaks and olive plantations, they will arrive at a coastline as beautiful as any in Europe, and one where blue skies are guaranteed for most of the year.

The mood of the country is as temperate as its climate. In a land caught between traditional living – fishing and farming – and the outside pressures of the rapidly encroaching modern world, people are for the most part gentle, courteous, hospitable to visitors, fatalistic and immensely tolerant.

Bom Jesus do Monte

In the hills of the north

Position and landscape

Look at a map and Portugal is a small rectangular strip of land in the southwest corner of the Iberian peninsula, bordered in the north and east by Spain, and in the south and west by the Atlantic Ocean. The total area of Portugal is 88,500sq km (34,360 sq miles) and this represents some 15 percent of the Iberian peninsula. The coastline extends for a total of 832km (516 miles). The Portuguese highlands in the northeast beneath the Spanish *meseta* slowly descend to the southwest. The Tagus (Spanish = *Tajo*, Portuguese = *Tejo*), the biggest river on the Iberian peninsula, cuts the country in half, separating the granite rock of the north (*Montanhas*) from the undulating south (*Planícies*). Important rivers such as the Minho and Douro have carved deep valleys between the northern mountain ranges. In the south a long stretch of the Guadiana forms the border with Spain.

The Serra da Estrêla

Despite the relatively small area, Portugal offers a quite unbelievable range of landscapes. In the north, visitors will find unspoilt wooded mountains dotted with lakes (now National Parks), a green coast bordered by pine trees (Costa Verde), the fertile market garden region by the Minho and the rugged and remote land 'behind the mountains' (Trás-os-Montes).

Central Portugal is dominated by the jagged peaks of the Serra da Estrêla, some reaching nearly 2,000m (6,500ft), the famous wine-producing Dão Valley, the broad coastal lagoon (Ria) at Aveiro and the flat, fertile alluvial Tagus Plain (Lezírias). Southern Portugal has a quite different character. First the wide horizons of the Alentejo Plain, the country's bread basket, followed by the luxuriant Serra da Monchique, a protective shield for the southernmost Algarve region with the rocky Barlavento in the west and the flat, sandy Sotavento in the east.

Varying shades of suntan

Climate

The Atlantic determines the climate for the whole of Portugal. The proximity of the ocean keeps the temperature lower than at comparable latitudes in the Mediterranean. In addition, the Atlantic brings more rain and a generally more changeable weather pattern than further east. As the landscape changes, so does the weather. Some regions, such as the Costa do Sol north of Lisbon and the nearby Serra da Sintra, have a favourable micro-climate while, further north, rain and fog frequently affect the coastal regions, even in high summer. The remote Trás-os-Montes region is characterised by hot summers and extremely cold winters. Sufficient snow falls in the Serra da Estrêla to create a winter sports playground. While summer temperatures along the west coast are moderate, in the Alentejo Plain and in the Algarve it can sometimes be unbearably hot. But the Algarve's winter climate is inviting enough to tempt many northern Europeans away from their long, gloomy nights – on average the Algarve receives 3,000 hours of sun per year. Elsewhere in Portugal winter is cold and damp.

Botanical bonanza

Fauna and flora

A plethora of plant life will thrive where geography and climate vary so greatly. Every region of Portugal has its own botanical peculiarities. Lush green growth covers the north and the protected regions of central Portugal. In the Serra da Estrêla for example, the birch, at home in northern Europe, grows alongside the Mediterranean oleander. Forests of pines, oaks and chestnuts have given way in recent years to eucalyptus plantations. In the south, bush and scrub (*matos*), olives, cork oaks and chestnut oaks create a steppe-like landscape. The eucalyptus is gaining a

Jardim Episcopal, Castelo Branco

foothold here too. Bananas and sugar cane thrive in the sub-tropical conditions on the Algarve.

A number of nature reserves have been established where the aim is to protect ancient landscapes and threatened plant and animal species. The most important is the Peneda-Gerês National Park in the far north, but apart from the Serra da Estrêla, most other protected zones are either along the mountainous Spanish border (Serras de Montesinho, Malcata, São Mamede) or on the coast (sand dunes near Aveiro, Serra da Sintra, Serra da Arrabida, from Sines to Sagres on the west coast and the lagoons of the eastern Algarve). The wetlands of the Sado Delta south of Setúbal, the northern bank of the Tagus Delta and the Sapal region near Castro-Marim by the mouth of the Guadiana are all important bird breeding grounds. Lovers of gardens will derive considerable pleasure from the grounds of the *quintas* with their collections of rare tropical specie.

Population

Despite its position on the periphery of Europe, in the past Portugal was the destination of many different races. The native Lusitanians mixed freely with Phoenicians, Celts, Romans, Germanic tribes and Arabs. The Voyages of Discovery later brought immigrants from Asia and Africa, as well as many *mulattos*, the offspring of the Portuguese colonists. Xenophobia and racial prejudice are unfamiliar concepts to most Portuguese. Proof of this came in 1975, when Portuguese colonial rule in Mozambique and Angola collapsed. More than 700,000 refugees fled to safety in Portugal but they were treated as 'returners' (*retornados*) and successfully integrated into the community.

Nevertheless, the infrastructure was too fragile to accommodate the continuing wave of new arrivals and the slums of Lisbon (*bairros de lata*) are home to many thousands of black Africans living in abject poverty. The weak-

Shepherd near Bragança

ness of the Portuguese economy has led to the departure of about 3.5 million *emigrantes* – mainly to France, Brazil and South Africa. The motherland now sustains a population of just under 10 million. There is, however, a huge difference in density between the coastal regions where three-quarters of the population live and the interior, which is home to the remaining quarter.

While many people have gone abroad, Greater Lisbon (30 percent of the total population) and Oporto/Braga (27 percent) have also attracted country dwellers hoping to improve their living standards. The contrast between rich and poor continues to be quite striking. However, the longer-term effects of 1974's Carnation Revolution have produced a consumer-oriented middle class which is threatening the traditional class boundaries.

Religion

Hieronymite Monastery Gardens

Portugal is a Catholic country and after the *reconquista* the church of Rome, represented by monks and orders of knights, supported the monarchy and the feudal society. A miracle saved the church from loss of influence when the monarchy collapsed in 1910: on 13 May 1917 the Virgin Mary appeared before three peasant children, thus giving believers a new focus for their faith. The clerical-fascist dictatorship of Salazar declared Portugal to be a Catholic state and deliberately sought to create a national myth out of the Fatima cult. Despite the separation of church and state, the church still maintains a tight grip on the country's institutions.

Customs and festivals

Festival participant

The Portuguese love of festivals and carnivals is legendary. Saints' days provide the opportunity for the *festas* and *romarias*. *Feiras* (markets) are often associated with such festivities. In the north in particular, every small town has its own carnival traditions with music, dancing, noisy fireworks and special celebrations. The act of paying respect to Christian forefathers is often just a way of giving ancient fertility rites and miracle worship a respectable gloss. Witches, mermaids and werewolves play just as important a part as the Christian saints.

Economy

When Portugal joined the European Community in 1986 it was one of the poorest countries in Europe, and it has remained so. However, a reprivatisation programme started in 1989 in order to create a market economy, and a type of Marshall Plan for Portugal mapped out in Brussels, have both given the economy a massive boost. However, there are many structural problems that Portugal needs to address if it is ever to reach parity with the EU countries of northern Europe. The road network is being extended but no coherent strategy has emerged. Only Lisbon and Oporto are linked by a fast train service. Hi-tech projects have failed to attract investment. Up until now foreign interest has concentrated on labour-intensive work such as the production of shoes and textiles which now make up about a third of Portuguese exports. This approach works as long as wages remain low to compete with Hong Kong and the Far East. The biggest contributor to Portugal's foreign currency reserves in recent years has been tourism, with an increase of 1,000 percent in the last 20 years. Money sent to families at home by 'guest workers' abroad is also an important element.

The poor relative in Portugal's national economy continues to be agriculture. Although every fifth Portuguese worker earns his or her living from the land, Portugal still has to import about half of its food requirements. The farms are too small and there is a shortage of machinery and expertise. The situation in the fishing industry is equally depressing. The colourful boats used by Portuguese fishermen cannot begin to compete with the well-equipped floating fish factories that sail out of the northern Spanish ports.

Sagres fishing port

The forestry industry is now tied to meeting the demands of industry. Where once deciduous forests and olive groves grew, the *eucalyptus globulus* now reigns supreme. This tree provides the raw material for the production of cellulose, a commodity that now far outstrips Portugal's traditional exports of wine and cork.

Harvesting cork

Administration

Portugal's borders have not changed for almost 800 years. Since the fall of the 50-year Salazar dictatorship in 1974 after the Carnation Revolution, the country has been run by a parliamentary democracy along west European lines. The left-wing government of Mario Soares was voted out of office in 1986, and since then the country has been run by the right-wing economist Anibal Cavaco Silva.

The autonomously administered Atlantic islands of Madeira and the Azores form part of the Portuguese nation with Lisbon as the capital. The tiny outpost of Macão in the South China Sea is the last remnant of the Portuguese empire. It is to be ceded to China in 1999.

In 1975 Portugal was forced to loosen its links with its former colonies in Africa as they sought independence. Since then Portugal has found itself looking increasingly towards Europe.

The Portuguese provinces from north to south are as follows: Minho, Trás-os-Montes, Douro, Beira Alta, Beira Baixa, Beira Litoral, Estremadura, Ribatejo, Alto and Baixo Alentejo, Algarve.

Historical Highlights

1000–500BC Phoenicians establish trading posts and colonies in southern Portugal.

700–500 Celts introduce the Iron Age.

202 Carthaginian enclaves along the eastern and southern seaboards pass to the Romans after the Second Punic War.

202–137 Lusitania (roughly modern Portugal) is annexed and subjugated by the Romans. Viriatus leads rebellion against Roman occupation from Viseu but is murdered in 139.

AD406–18 Barbarian tribes, notably the Germanic Suebi, sweep over the Iberian peninsula.

469 Visigoths expel the Suebi and effectively establish their own kingdom in Portugal.

711 Moors invade from North Africa. The last Visigothic military resistance at Mérida (713) and Ossonoba (captured in 714).

8th century Relics of the 4th-century martyr St Vincent brought to the sacred promontory of Cape St Vincent.

1064 County of Coimbra established by Ferdinand, Count of Castile.

1095 Alfonso VI of Leon and Castile entrusts Henry of Burgundy with the enlarged county of Coimbra, now called 'Portucale'.

1114 Alfonso Henriques declares an independent nation of Portugal from Minho to Modego, with Coimbra as the capital.

1147 Alfonso and Crusaders conquer the Moorish stronghold of Lisbon.

1173 St Vincent's relics taken to Lisbon. Legend has it that the boat bore a raven fore and aft which became the crest of Lisbon.

1185 Sancho I begins conquest of the remaining Moslem-held territory in the south.

1248 Alfonso III musters forces for a further campaign against the troublesome Moors.

1249 Moors finally driven out of Faro and Silves.

1385 Fernando I dies, ending the Burgundian dynasty. Juan I of Castile prepares to invade, whereupon João of the House of Avis is appointed as Defender of the Realm. In the same year the Portuguese army under João of Avis routs Castilians at the battle of Aljubarrota and João becomes King João I. He marries Philippa of Lancaster, daughter of John of Gaunt, who had previously made claims to the throne of Castile.

1386 The Treaty of Windsor formalises the alliance between England and Portugal.

1415 Portuguese forces under Prince Henry the Navigator take Ceuta in Morocco, marking the beginning of Portuguese colonial expansion. Madeira, Azores and Cape Verde Islands follow.

1488 Bartolomeu Dias rounds the Cape of Good Hope.

1495 Manuel I ascends the throne.

1497–8 Vasco da Gama opens the sea route to India.

1500 Pedro Alvares Cabral discovers Brazil and the Spice Islands.

1520 Magellan sets out on his voyage to circumnavigate the globe.

1543 Portuguese establish contact with the Japanese.

1557 Portuguese merchants found the colony of Macão. Sebastião ascends the throne.

1578 The disappearance of the heirless King Sebastião after his defeat at the Battle of the Three Kings in Morocco leaves Portugal without a ruler. This marks the end of Portugal's supremacy.

1580 Phillip II of Spain invades and annexes Portugal, which becomes a Spanish province.

1589 Sir Francis Drake fails in his attempt to capture Lisbon.

1607–30 Portugal loses part of her empire during Spanish rule.

1640 The nationalist revolution brings Spanish rule to an end. The Duke of Bragança becomes King João IV of Portugal.

1662 Catherine of Bragança marries Charles II of England. Tangier and Bombay are part of her dowry.

1703 British influence results in the Methuen Treaty with unfavourable consequences for the Portuguese economy.

1755 The Great Earthquake destroys Lisbon. Marquês de Pombal rebuilds city centre.

1807 French invasion under Junot. Portuguese royal family escape to Brazil in English ships.

1808 Peninsula War begins, with the Portuguese army supporting Wellington.

1810 Massena is prevented from entering Lisbon by the lines of Torres Vedras.

1811 The French leave Portugal.

1821 Royal family returns, following the intervention of the British.

1832–4 War of the Two Brothers, between Miguel (Liberals) and Pedro (Absolutists) for the Crown.

1891 Unsuccessful Republican revolt.

1892 Country declared bankrupt.

1901 British, French and German representatives control national budget.

1903 Treaty of Windsor is publicly reaffirmed during a visit by Edward VII to Portugal.

1908 King Carlos assassinated by fanatics.

1910 Portugal declared a republic. Manuel II is forced to abdicate and flees to England.

1916 Portugal enters World War I against Germany. Economic problems continue.

1926 The Gomes da Costa dictatorship begins, followed by a coup d'état after which Carmona becomes president.

1928 António de Oliveira Salazar is appointed Minister of Finance to restore economic order.

1932 Salazar becomes Prime Minister, retaining the financial portfolio.

1933 Salazar announces a new constitution granting himself dictatorial powers.

1939–45 Portugal, while remaining neutral in the war, leases the Azores to the USA, thereby helping to defeat German submarines.

1949 Portugal joins NATO.

1955 Portugal joins United Nations.

1960 Opposition to Salazar grows.

1968 Salazar retires on the grounds of ill health and Marcelo Caetano takes over and begins a policy of liberalisation.

1974 Dictatorship is overthrown in a bloodless coup d'état, known as the Carnation Revolution.

1974–5 Portuguese colonies in Africa win independence, and some 700,000 refugees pour into Portugal.

1976 A constitution is drawn up based on universal suffrage and a single legislative chamber. Socialists win the election and Dr Mario Soares becomes Prime Minister of a minority government, which survives with the help of a series of coalitions until 1980.

1982 Soares returned to power after a centre-right alliance under Francisco Pinto Balsemão falters.

1985– Centre-right government under Anibal Cavaco Silva.

1986 Portugal joins the EC. Soares becomes Portugal's first civilian president in 60 years. He is reelected in 1991.

1994 Lisbon is the cultural capital of Europe.

View of the Baixa
Preceding pages: an enduring mode of transport

Route 1

Lisbon – The White City

Lisbon, the capital of Portugal, enjoys a marvellous position. To the northeast of the city the River Tagus opens out to form the glistening Mar de Palha (Sea of Straw). The city stands on the northwest bank of this lake just before it narrows and flows out into the Atlantic Ocean. For several miles, homes, factories, warehouses and port installations carpet the steep hills and valleys along the estuary. The best view of the *Cidade Branca*, the White City – the predominant colour is really a matt pastel shade – can be enjoyed from one of the many excellent fish restaurants in Cacilhas on the south bank of the river. Between Alfama, the labyrinth of narrow alleys on the citadel hill, and the elevated Bairro Alto, lies the flat plain of the city centre, the Cidade Baixa, with its geometrical street plan. Leading down to the Baixa is the wide, tree-lined Avenida da Liberdade. Old trams, the *eléctricos*, wind their noisy way along the inclines of the narrow streets. Funicular railways or *elevadores* and an unusual lift with an elaborate neo-Gothic exterior negotiate the steep inclines of one of the hilliest harbour towns in the world. Lisbon's many *miradouros* or panoramas provide spectacular views over the river and the town, but a tour of the city will also reveal many otherwise hidden sights. Just a few yards from the roar of city traffic, steep flights of steps disappear into sleepy corners where caged birds sing. Idyllic parks with exotic plants and peaceful waters are a refuge from the hectic hurly-burly of the city streets.

In Alfama

Between the huge, post-modern towers of the Amoreiras Shopping Center, towering symbols of Lisbon's share in the prosperity of modern Europe, and the tiny buildings with doll's house facades in the old town, there are examples – small and large – of many different styles of architecture. Lisbon has resisted the melancholic decadence and so-called myth of progress of the late 20th century. All the senses are required to appreciate Lisbon's busy street life with its confusing variety of shops, bars, sounds and smells.

History

From very early times the large natural harbour at the mouth of the Tagus has been a centre for trade. The name derives from the Phoenicians who called the place 'Alis-Ubbo' or 'Lovely Bay'. Greeks and Romans named the port 'Olisipo' after Ulysses who was said to have founded the city. The Romans gained control of the town and it was renamed 'Felicitas Julia' after the emperor Julius Caesar, but, 300 years later, power was ceded to tribes of Germanic peoples, Alans, Vandals and Visigoths, although they were expelled by the Arabs or Moors in 715. They expanded the town of 'Lishbuna' and much evidence of their 400-year rule remains.

In 1147 the first Portuguese king, Alfonso Henriques, conquered the city and 100 years later it became the capital of the kingdom. Lisbon's years of prosperity started around the end of the 15th century when, as a result of the Voyages of Discovery, Portugal became Europe's first colonial power. During the reign of Manuel I (1425–1521), it is said that every year 2,000 ships unloaded precious goods from Africa, India and South America at the docks along the banks of the Tagus. Lisbon became the richest city in Europe. However, hardly a stone remains from Lisbon's heyday. On 1 November 1755 the worst earthquake ever to strike a European city destroyed a large part of the capital and killed 40,000 inhabitants. The rest of Europe found it hard to comprehend the scale of the disaster and philosophers such as Voltaire and Kant were preoccupied by the meaning of this catastrophe. By chance, the levers of power at that time were in the hands of one of Portugal's most able statesmen, the Marquês de Pombal. Not only did he set in train a rapid and well-planned reconstruction of the city but also a thorough modernisation of the mechanisms of power in accordance with the principles of Benevolent Despotism. One of Pombal's lasting legacies is the Cidade Baixa – its network of right-angled streets and the uniform blocks of housing remain largely unaltered. Some destruction to the city occurred during the Napoleonic invasion of 1807 and the dissolution of religious orders in 1834 led to the closure of 65 monasteries. Some were converted into barracks but many were allowed to decay. From the middle of the 19th century onwards, steps were taken to improve and extend

Shopping in Alfama

King Alfonso

Park Eduardo VII, Avenidas Novas

the city in a grand style. One of the first measures was to create a new boulevard to the north, the Avenida da Liberdade, followed by other grand thoroughfares. Public parks, theatres and libraries were built to satisfy the needs of Lisbon's expanding middle classes. In the 1930s and 1940s the government of the dictator Salazar constructed public buildings, squares and a new quarter, the Alvalade, near these Avenidas Novas. The dominant style in these new areas could be described as art deco but it shared some similarities with the Fascist-inspired architecture prevalent in Italy and Germany during the 1930s.

The city's development plan also included the creation of a modern traffic network which required the compulsory purchase of large expanses of private property. The trees planted on the Monsanto hill in the west of the city

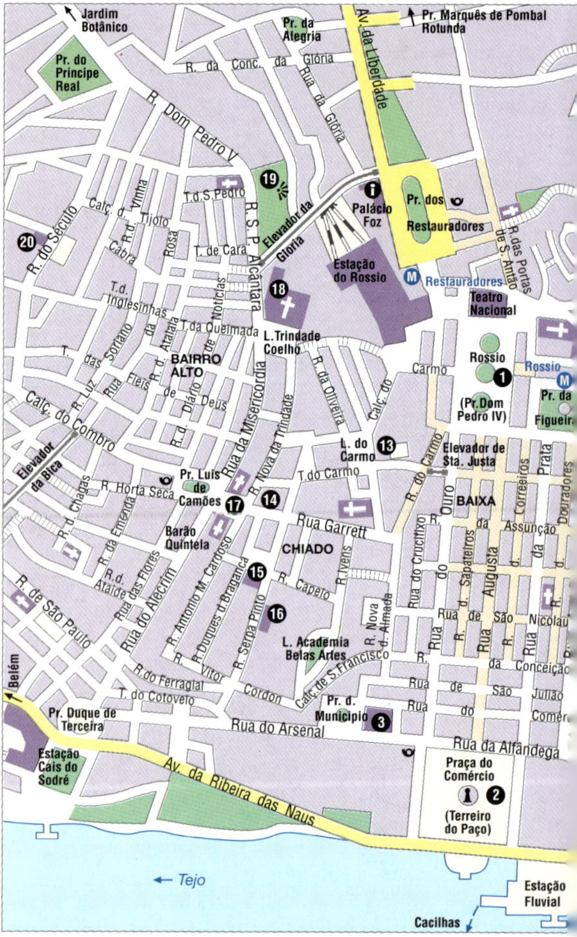

and the housing estates, the *bairros sociais*, are among the most valued legacies of the Salazar years. In 1966, shortly before he started to lose his grip on power, a majestic suspension bridge across the Tagus was built. It was named the Ponte de 25 de Abril or simply O Ponte to commemorate the start of the revolution that eventually brought a democratically-elected government to power. Building speculation has led to unplanned development in the hinterland and much of the old housing stock has been allowed to fall into disrepair. Rents are still based on levels established in 1943.

Bairros de lata or shanty towns, populated mainly by black Africans from Portugal's former colonies, exist on the edge of the city. It is estimated that about 900,000 people live within the city's boundaries but, if the Greater Lis-

Ramshackle housing in Alfama

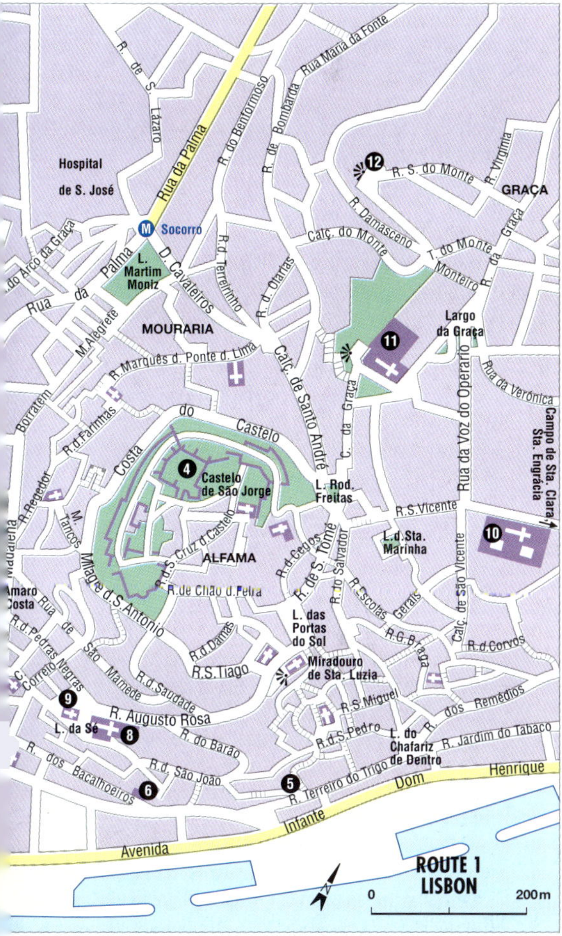

bon conurbation, which extends as far as Setubal, is included, then the population is nearer three million.

Sights

A tour of Lisbon is best completed on foot and, with many steep inclines and smooth limestone cobbles underfoot, it is advisable to wear a stout pair of shoes. Maps can be misleading, as the steep hills create a false impression of the distances involved. However, many visitors may find it more rewarding simply to go with the crowd and observe the many-sided mosaic of Lisbon life in a haphazard way, rather than rush from one monument to the next.

Rossío Station

Rossío

The **Rossío** ❶, a large square surrounded by café tables, is the heart of Lisbon and serves as a good starting point for tours of the town. Heretics were burnt at the stake here and it was also a venue for bullfights. In the middle of the traffic-free island stand two fountains and a statue of Dom Pedro IV, hence its official name **Praça de Dom Pedro IV**. Around the edge are a number of celebrated cafés such as the art deco **Nicola** or the popular **Pastelaria Suiça**. Both are ideal places to sit and observe the multi-ethnic nature of modern Lisbon. Indian, African and Asiatic features in the faces of the passers-by reflect Portugal's maritime history and status as a colonial power. It is worth taking a peep inside the tiny **Tabacaria Monaco** next to the Nicola. This tobacconist and newspaper stand retains the original 1894 furnishings. Portugal's national theatre, the Classical **Teatro Nacional Dona Maria II,** stands on the north side of the Rossío and occupies the site of the former Palace of the Inquisition. The decorative mosaics pieced together from white limestone and black basalt that can be seen on the pavements and squares in the city centre are the work of former convicts.

Café Nicola

Baixa

The orderly street plan of the Baixa, the result of Pombal's grand scheme to rebuild the city after the 1755 earthquake, stands in stark contrast to the rest of the city centre where narrow streets wind and merge with no particular pattern. There is no other part of the old town where the right angle is so dominant. Pombal left no room for palaces and churches. The buildings were intended as town houses for the middle classes and as outlets for traders such as jewellers and cloth and leather suppliers. The street names testify to the district's past. **Rua dos Sapateiros** near the Rossío was the shoemakers' street. The **Animatógrafo do Rossío** here was established in 1907 and was Lisbon's first cinema. Note the flourishes of the art nouveau facade. The stuccoed café **Leitaria A Camponesa** at No 155 dates from the same period. **Rua Augusta** is now a pedestrianised zone and at No 44–52 stands a house that has not changed since the Pombal years. Pombal's houses were built with a cage-like timber framework capable of withstanding any future earthquake, and, if a similar disaster occurs again, they will fare better than the modern multistorey blocks which have been designed without any consideration given to the possibility of earthquakes.

Elevador de Santa Justa

Parallel to Rua Augusta run the streets for the gold and silversmiths, **Rua do Ouro** and **Rua da Prata**. The **Chá-Vianna-Café** at No 61 in Rua da Prata is another place for lovers of nostalgia. It is a genuine grocer's store from the middle of the last century. **Rua Santa Justa** runs at right angles to Rua Augusta and at the end stands the neo-Gothic tower for the **Elevador de Santa Justa** lift which links the low-lying Baixa with the Carmo district (*see page 24*). The Baixa remains dedicated to meeting the needs of merchants and traders and is largely a financial and commercial district.

The southern end of Rua Augusta finishes with a triumphal arch that opens on to **Praça do Comércio** ❷. This square is surrounded by arcades on three sides. In the days before the earthquake Manuel I's royal palace was located here and this square is still sometimes referred to as **Terreiro do Paço** (Palace Square). In the middle stands a baroque equestrian statue of the reform-minded king José I, who gave the Marquês de Pombal a free hand to rebuild the city after the earthquake. Unfortunately the square, which overlooks the Tagus and thus symbolises Lisbon's historic links with the oceans has lost much of its splendour as it is currently used as a car park. In the northeast corner of the square (No 3) lies the historic **Martinho**

King José I and Praça do Comércio

Pelourinho

da Arcada café, which is now an expensive restaurant. It used to be the haunt of Fernando Pessoa, a renowned Lisbon poet who is said to have enjoyed a bottle of cognac there every day.

Opposite the restaurant stands Lisbon's General Post Office. It was here in 1908, two years before a republic was declared, that King Carlos I and his heir, Luís Filipe, were brutally murdered. Right behind it is the 19th-century **Town Hall** (Município) ❸. On Town Hall Square stands a twisting column known as the **Pelourinho**. Used in the past as a pillory, it remains as a symbol of municipal jurisdiction.

Situated by the Tagus on the east side of Praça do Comércio is the **Terminal Fluvial**. Ferries leave from here for the other side of the river. Warehouses and docks extend along the banks of the river for about 20km (12 miles). It is no longer the shipyard where the famous Portuguese caravels were built, but a ship repair yard for oil tankers. **Lisnave** and **Setenave** on the other side of the river are the biggest ship repair yards in the world.

To the west of Praça do Comércio lies the **Estacão Cais do Sodré**, the station that serves the suburbs between Lisbon and **Cascais** and the departure point for ferries to the other side of the river.

Roof decoration in Alfama

Castelo de São Jorge

Alfama

To the east of the Baixa at the foot of the citadel hill stands the oldest quarter of the town. The houses here were built on rock and therefore survived the worst of the earthquake. This part of the town was inhabited by the Romans. On the corner of Rua São Mamede and Rua da Saudade the remains of a theatre have been unearthed. It later became the Arab quarter and the Jews also resided here but they were expelled in the 16th century. The **Castelo de São Jorge** ❹ and its predecessors have served to guard the mouth of the river, but the ruins which were restored during the Salazar regime show few details of the Alcáçova, once the king's residence and the scene for great celebrations after Vasco da Gama's voyage to India. It is, none the less, the finest *miradouro* in the capital with views over the whole city and river.

The alleyways of Alfama, which wind their way anarchically around the slopes at the foot of the castle hill, lead into another world. Steep hills and long flights of steps keep traffic at bay. The smell of exhaust fumes is replaced by the aroma of grilling sardines. No noisy diesel engines, instead the twittering of canaries and the cackle of chicken mingle with the banter of women selling fish and vegetables on the street corners. Tourists find it hard to resist the wine bars and cheap restaurants.

The main Alfama thoroughfare is **Rua de São Pedro**. From the western end by the Largo de São Rafael, cut through Rua Judiaria to the **Largo do Terreiro do Trigo** with the **Chafariz d'El Rei** ❺, Lisbon's oldest public fountain. The use of the various water sources was strictly regulated according to social class. A decree in 1551 stated precisely when and where mulattos, convicts, Indians, coloured slaves, white women and girls, galley slaves and soldiers could draw water. The city's corn was stored in the huge **Celeiro do Trigo** warehouses opposite the fountain. The 23 tram passes here on its way out of town to **Santa Apolónia** station and then on to the **Madre de Deus museum**. Returning to the city centre, it passes along **Rua dos Bacalheiros** and the 16th-century **Casa dos Bicos** ❻ with its extravagant 'diamond' facade, before reaching **Praça do Comércio**. In Rua da Alfândega, the Manueline facade of the **Conceiçao Velha church** ❼ is also worth closer inspection.

To visit upper Alfama, tired walkers may prefer to use the famous 28 tram which runs between **Rua da Conceição** in the Baixa and **Graça**.

The first stop is Lisbon's medieval cathedral, the **Sé** ❽ (from the Latin *sedes episcopalis* meaning 'bishop's seat'). Built on a slope over the site of a mosque, it served as a monument to the Christian victory over the Moors. It was badly damaged in the earthquake and then rebuilt. It is still an impressive testimony to the church builders who worked during the early years of the Portuguese monarchy. The tall, dark main nave is predominantly Romanesque, while the ambulatory is in simple Gothic style. Apart from the 18th-century **nativity crib** in the first chapel on the left of the entrance and a number of Gothic **tombstones** in the ambulatory chapels, there is little of special note, although the Gothic arch and Romanesque wrought-iron screen in the **crossing** are worth looking out for.

The small church of **Santo Antonio da Sé** ❾ with its baroque gable lies beneath the Sé. It is dedicated to St Antonius of Padua, who became known locally as St Anthony of Lisbon. He was apparently born nearby and has since become the city's favourite saint. On 13 June every year, a grand festival is held in his honour.

The next stop on the tram route is the famous **Miradouro de Santa Luzia**, a viewing terrace with a shady pergola and brightly tiled benches at the rear of the church of the same name. **Travessa de Santa Luzia** opposite leads up towards the Castelo de São Jorge. Just around the corner lies the pretty **Largo das Portas do Sol** with an array of pavement cafés. Its name is derived from a gate in the Moorish city wall. The view from here over the roofs of Alfama, the river and the white church domes matches the view from the *miradouro*.

Casa dos Bicos

Cathedral vaulting

Miradouro de Santa Luzia

The next stop is at the church of **São Vicente de Fora** ⓾, once situated outside the city walls. This severe late Renaissance building with a dominant twin tower facade is in Spanish/Italian style. Dating from the Spanish occupation, it was built on the orders of Philip II and consecrated in 1629. The cloisters in the adjoining monastery are covered with 18th-century *azulejo* frescoes, many of which illustrate La Fontaine's fables. The graves of the members of the Bragança dynasty can also be seen nearby.

To the east of São Vicente lies **Campo de Santa Clara** with some fine patrician houses, a 19th-century market hall and the **Feira da Ladra**, Lisbon's oldest but not necessarily its most interesting flea market (Tuesday morning and Saturday). Beneath the square rises the huge white dome of the Santa Engrácia church. Work started 500 years ago, but it wasn't completed until 1966. *Obras de Santa Engrácia* is an expression used to describe something that takes an eternity to complete – not unusual in Portugal. Salazar demanded that the building be completed as a pantheon to honour Portugal's national heroes. In side apses beneath the vast dome stand six empty tombstones, engraved simply with the names of the great men. The tram continues its journey up **Rua Voz do Operario** (named after a 100-year-old working men's club) north of São Vicente into the working-class quarter of **Graça**. Of particular interest here are some *vilas*, workers' flats built at the turn of the century. They are grouped around courtyards and equipped with external staircases. Notable examples are **Vila Sousa**, in the rear courtyard of No 82 Largo da Graça, and **Vila Berta** at Rua do Sol à Graça 55–9, decorated with *azulejos*. The district has two ★ **mi-**

Statue of St Vincent and interior detail of São Vicente de Fora

radouros offering superb views of the city: one is the café terrace in front of the **Graça church** ⓫; the other stands on a hill by the **Nossa Senhora do Monte chapel** ⓬. The tram returns to the Baixa from Largo da Graça or continues on to **Martim Moniz** beneath the northern slopes of the Castelo de São Jorge by **Mouraria**, the old Moorish quarter.

Avenida da Liberdade

Avenida da Liberdade

Lisbon's Champs Elysées is 1.5km (1 mile) long and 100m (325ft) wide. It starts at the northwest corner of the Rossío by the Rossío station (*Estacão do Rossío*) with its Moorish/Manueline facade. Trains from here serve Sintra and intermediate suburbs. **Praça dos Restauradores** lies at this end of the boulevard and Lisbon's main tourist office, is situated in the pink-washed **Palácio Foz**. Bookings for everything from cinema tickets to bullfights are available from a kiosk nearby. Lisbon still has a number of old-style cinema halls such as the protected 1930s **Eden** on the west side of the square. **Rua das Portas de Santo Antão** behind the east side of the square is a street with fish restaurants, the **Odeon** cinema, the 1913 **Politeama** and the multi-purpose stage in the *belle epoque* **Coliseu**.

The start of work on Avenida da Liberdade in 1879 was the first stage of a large-scale extension of the city, but unfortunately building development in recent years has resulted in the demolition of rows of fine houses built at the turn of the century and the construction of faceless squares that could be anywhere in the world. Banks, offices and fashion shops now occupy these prime sites rather than fine blocks of flats and town houses. A stroll up the Avenida as far as **Praça Marquês de Pombal** will take about half an hour. This important junction, which is more often referred to as the **Rotunda**, is actually a roundabout centred around a statue of the reformer. Many important thoroughfares meet here. Avenida Fontes Pereira de Melo branches off to the northeast to the **Avenidas Novas** and the **Campo Grande** while Avenida Joaquim A. de Aguiar forks to the west and links up with the motorway network. Just before the motorway access road stands the huge **Amoreiras Shopping Center** with its glass towers symbolising Lisbon's new prosperity.

Amoreiras Shopping Center

On the hill to the north of the Rotunda lies the **Parque Eduardo VII**. Some of Lisbon's top hotels are to be found on its western edge while the terrace at the upper end serves as a ★★ **miradouro** with a unique view over the Avenida da Liberdade and the River Tagus. Just below lies the ★ **Estufa Fria**, a 'cold greenhouse' in an old quarry where tropical plants thrive amid ponds and running water (daily 10am–6pm, in winter 10am–5pm).

Estufa Fria

Chiado and the Bairro Alto

The ruins of the Carmo church

Take the **Elevador de Santa Justa** (*see page 19*) from the Baixa into the upper town. This ornate lift was built in 1902 and overcomes a difference in height of about 32m (105ft). From the upper exit and the **Chiado Mel** restaurant, there is a marvellous ★ **view** of the Rossío and the grid layout of the Baixa. Close to the steep precipice lie the towering ruins of the Gothic **Carmo church** ⓭, the last memorial to the victims of the earthquake and now also the **Archaeological Museum** (Tuesday to Saturday 10am–1pm, 2–5pm, in summer 10am–6pm).

The road from **Largo do Carmo** with its baroque fountain and flocks of pigeons descends to **Chiado**, the old literary quarter. Monuments and streets here are dedicated to famous Portuguese poets and writers. Old-fashioned cafés such as **A Brasileira** ⓮ and **Pastelaria Bénard** in Rua Garrett, antique shops and antiquarian booksellers such as **Livraria Bernard** (established 1732), **São Carlos opera house** ⓯ and other theatres all help to create an artistic atmosphere. The district has been given a cultural boost by the 1994 opening of the **Museo do Chiado** ⓰ in Rua Serpa Pinto (Tuesday 2–6pm, Wednesday to Sunday 10am–6pm), an architecturally interesting museum housing Portuguese art from the late 19th century to the present day. Chiado is now a busy shopping area with **Rua Garrett** and **Rua do Carmo** the main axes. A stroll past the shop windows will reveal exquisitely elegant interiors with ornamental plasterwork, paintings and mirrored glass cabinets.

A Brasileira

At the lower end of Rua Garrett, the ugly scar left by the 1988 fire can still be seen. Contrary to media reports at the time, it was not the whole of the old town that suffered, but 18 fine, historic houses were destroyed. Lisbon has had no fewer than 21 large fires this century. At the upper end lies **Largo do Chiado** ⓱ where two churches face each other and also **Largo Luís de Camões**, a square surrounded by elms which is dedicated to the famous Portuguese poet.

São Roque

The late Renaissance church of ★ **São Roque** ⓲ which is situated in **Praça Trindade Coelho** at the northern end of both Rua da Misericórdia and Rua Nova da Trindade was largely spared by the earthquake. The structure of this Jesuit church is restrained, although the interior contains some artistic decorative work. The 16th-century *azulejo* walls in the porch and the third chapel on the right are probably the most interesting features. **Capela de São João**, the fourth on the left, dates from 1742 and was extravagantly finished in gold and jewels imported from Rome on the instructions of João V.

A number of bars and cafés in the vicinity will provide not only welcome refreshment but another glimpse into Lisbon's past. **Cervejaria da Trindade** (Rua Nova da Trindade 20) is a traditional beer hall housed in an old monastery with some fine 19th-century *azulejo* walls. The **Instituto do Vinho do Porto** or Port Wine Institute (daily 10am–10pm) is housed in the **Casa Ludovice** at Rua S. Pedro de Alcântara 45. This mansion was designed in 1747 by the Mafra architect Johann Friedrich Ludwig (*see page 86*). Over 100 different types of port can be sampled here at very reasonable prices (Monday to Saturday 10am –10pm). The Miradouro **São Pedro de Alcântara** ⓳, diagonally opposite, provides a fine view of the city. The **Elevador da Gloria** cable car nearby has been carrying passengers up and down between the upper town and Praça dos Restauradores for over a hundred years. Rua Dom Pedro V is one of Lisbon's main antiques centres. On the corner with Rua da Rosa stands a superb *belle epoque* bakery known as the **Padaria Italiana** and it is well worth a look. Hidden away behind No 89 is **Pavilhão Cinês**, an amusingly furnished bar occupying an old chemist's shop. The road ends by the **Principe Real**, a pretty garden with a Goa cedar which provides more than enough shade for the card players. Lisbon's **Botanical Gardens** are only a few minutes' walk away. The entrance is on the right-hand side of the **Escola Politécnica** in the street of the same name. The gardens were opened in 1858 and can now boast two huge dragon trees and an avenue of palm trees which contains 35 different varieties.

The return journey passes through the **Bairro Alto**, which lies further west and has **Rua da Rosa** as one of its main thoroughfares. This quarter was planned as a residential area in the 16th century and, after Alfama, is the second-oldest part of the city. The quarter to the east of Rua da Rosa enjoys a lively atmosphere with small shops and simple bars known as *tascas* at street level. Above, the crumbling plaster is masked by washing blowing in the breeze, while flowerpots and bird cages adorn the balconies.

The Bairro Alto is an important centre for Lisbon's nightlife. Restaurants, bars, lively discos and *fado* bars keep both locals and tourists entertained. A variety of restaurants and snack bars here are kept busy particularly at lunchtime serving the *pratos de dia*, a low-price dish of the day. **Pap'Açorda** at Rua da Atal aia 57–9 is very popular and it is advisable to reserve a table.

The side of Bairro Alto west of Rua da Rosa has a quite different character. The quiet **Rua do Século** contains the **Palácio dos Carvalhos** ⓴, where Pombal was born in 1699, a baroque square and fountain and a beautiful building constructed in 1913 for the editorial offices of the *O Século* newspaper. Largo de Camões serves as the boundary between the Bairro Alto and Chiado.

Cervejaria da Trindade

View from São Pedro de Alcântara

Never far to a fado bar

Estrêla and Lapa

Basilica da Estrêla

Henry the Navigator in the famous polyptych

Take the 28 tram again, but this time in the direction of Estrêla and Prazeres. Catch the tram in either **Rua da Conceição** in the Baixa or in the **Largo do Chiado**, from where it curves past the **Bento Palace**, seat of the National Assembly, and then continues up to the Estrêla hill, which is crowned by the **Basilica da Estrêla**, a domed basilica with twin towers of white limestone. It was commissioned by Queen Maria II on the birth of the heir to the throne and was consecrated in 1787, one of Europe's last baroque churches and similar in design to Mafra (*see page 35*). The sarcophagus of the founder who died insane lies to the left of the high altar. The view from the dome (*zimborio*) is quite stunning. Opposite the church the shady **Jardim da Estrêla** with its pool and elegant music pavilion (*coreto*) is the perfect spot for a quiet rest. At the tram terminus lies the **Cemitério dos Prazeres**, the 11-ha (27-acre) western cemetery, an unusual town in miniature as the tombs of the dead are copies of their homes.

The residential district beneath the Estrêla Basilica, known as **Lapa**, was originally inhabited by African slaves, but wealthy English families appreciated the fine view over the river and built grand villas here. The Portuguese aristocracy followed, but the district is now favoured by foreign embassies and the wealthy. Walk downhill and admire the fine houses, some of which date from the 18th century. Very attractive gardens lie hidden behind the high walls. To explore the Lapa quarter, first walk up Rua de João de Deus near the Estrêla church. From then on, follow Rua dos Navigantes downhill into Rua de Buenos Aires and Rua de São Domingos à Lapa. The area around here and **Rua do Sacramento à Lapa** is the smartest in Lapa. Rua do São Domingos à Lapa ends near a baroque fountain on **Rua das Janelas Verdes**.

Situated opposite is the ★★ **Museu Nacional de Arte Artiga** (Tuesday to Sunday 10am–1pm, 2.30 5pm), the most important museum in Lisbon after the Gulbenkian Museum (*see page 29*). Many of the finest exhibits here are Portuguese paintings of the 15th and 16th centuries that were influenced by the great Flemish artists, but the highlight is undoubtedly the polyptych from St Vincent's altar. Painted in about 1480 by Nuno Gonçalves, it shows Henry the Navigator and his contemporaries. Hieronymus Bosch's triptych of *The Temptation of St Anthony* is another of the museum's masterpieces.

Rua das Janelas Verdes was for many centuries the main road to Belém, as the Tagus came right to the foot of the hill. The whole area by the riverbank was cleared in the 19th century to make way for road, railway and port installations. The 15 and 17 trams still follow the old route to Belém, leaving from Praça do Comércio.

The Hieronymite Monastery

Belém

★★★ **Belém** lies at the western end of Greater Lisbon and can be reached by train from the **Cais do Sodré** station (note: express trains do not stop in Belém), by bus, taxi or the 15 or 17 tram.

The ★★★ **Mosteiro dos Jerónimos** or Hieronymite Monastery in Belém is by far the most interesting building in Lisbon. The monastery and Torre de Belém watchtower (*see page 29*) are unique memorials to Portugal's Golden Age, which followed after the Voyages of Discovery. Both buildings survived the earthquake.

The No 15 tram to Belém

The long side of the monastery now overlooks lawns and gardens, but the complex originally stood by the water's edge near Restelo harbour, from where the Portuguese explorers set sail in their caravels. Before the monastery was built, a small chapel existed on the site and it was in this chapel that Vasco da Gama prayed before leaving for India in July 1497 and where Manuel I welcomed him back in September 1499. With the discovery of a sea route to India, the king commissioned the building of a monastery on the site of the chapel and the foundation stone was laid in 1500. It was not finished at the time of the king's death in 1521. Work stopped in 1572 and the project was never completed, a fate shared by many other grand schemes. Consequently, the building cannot be attributed to any one architect but Boytac and João de Castilho were most influential in its design.

Manueline masterpiece

One of the most striking features of the monastery is the ★ **south doorway**. Like a huge monstrance it rises to a height of 32m (105ft) and it is the most ornate entrance of the Manueline period. The intricate designs, depicting scenes from the life of St Hieronymus, are the work of João Castilho, the famous Manueline architect.

The main entrance lies almost hidden away under the west porch. The ★ **west doorway** is the work of the

Frenchman **Nicolas de Chanterène** (*see page 85*) and it shows King Manuel I and his wife Maria of Castile, kneeling in the company of St Hieronymus and John the Baptist, beneath scenes from Bethlehem (Belém).

The fan vaulting of the interior

The finely ornamented ★★ **interior** is surprisingly wide. The late-Gothic nave and side aisles measure 92m (302ft) from the west doorway to the choir in the east. It is 22m (72ft) wide and 25m (82ft) high. The roof is supported by octagonal columns only 1m (3ft) in diameter and covered with delicate Renaissance embellishments, with Gothic fan vaulting overhead. Even bolder is the apparently unsupported structure above the transept with vaulting stretching 29m (95ft) from the crossing pillars as far as the choir wall. The plain Renaissance choir, a marble pantheon, where the sarcophagi of Manuel I, his son João III and their wives rest on stone elephants, stands in stark contrast to the ornamented nave. In the southern section an empty grave awaits the last king of the Avis dynasty, Sebastião, who disappeared in Morocco. The poet Luís de Camões, who died of the plague and was buried in a mass grave, is commemorated by an empty sarcophagus. The tomb of another Portuguese hero, Vasco da Gama, can also be found here under the gallery.

The ★★★ **cloisters** rank among the finest examples of Manueline architecture. Form and harmony were not the principle requirements, rather enchantment and exhilaration. With arches reflected in a pool, it resembled a palace courtyard for an extravagant prince and his courtiers more than a walkway for devout monks.

Padrão dos Descobrimentos

Two museums have been opened in the monastery: the **Museu da Marinha** (Maritime Museum) with model ships and the Museu **Nacional de Arqueologia e Etnologia** (Museum of Archaeology and Ethnology).

Opposite the monastery and beside the Tagus stands the **Padrão dos Descobrimentos** or Monument to the Discoveries. It dates from 1960 and was commissioned by Salazar to commemorate the 500th anniversary of the death of Henry the Navigator. Further to the west the **Museu de Arte Popular** (Museum of Popular Art) stands on the edge of a lake.

Flowers in the Jardim do Ultramar

Restaurants line **Rua de Belém** which leads away from the monastery into the town centre. Look out for the **Fábrica dos Pasteis de Belém**, a traditional café where the renowned speciality *Pasteis de Belém* has been made since 1837. On the corner of Calçada de Galvão is the entrance to the **Jardim do Ultramar**, a small peaceful park with a number of exotic plants. **Rua Vieira Portuense**, which runs parallel to Rua de Belém, contains a number of splendid town houses dating from the 16th and 17th centuries. The pink **Palácio de Belém** at the end of Rua de Belém is the official residence of the Portuguese president. An old royal riding school is now used to house the **Museu Nacional dos Coches** or Coach Museum. Many other grand buildings nearby, including the **Royal Ajuda Palace** higher up, testify to the important role of Belém in Portugal's Golden Age.

The ★★ **Torre de Belém,** a few minutes' walk upstream, is a major landmark. This Manueline bastion was conceived as a lighthouse and fortress and lay offshore, but it is now linked to the land. King Miguel incarcerated his political opponents in the dungeon as recently as the 19th century. The turrets bear the Cross of the Knights of Christ and the tiny towers at each corner are thought to have been influenced by Indian architecture. The view from the 35-m (115-ft) high terrace should not be missed.

Torre de Belém

Additional sights

★★★ **Museu Calouste Gulbenkian**, Avenida da Berna 45, tel: 793 5131 (June to September, Tuesday, Thursday, Friday, Sunday 10am–5pm, Wednesday and Saturday 2–7.30pm; October to May, Tuesday to Sunday 10am–5pm), is the most famous art museum in Portugal. When the Armenian oil magnate Gulbenkian died in 1955, he bequeathed his estate to the Portuguese people, partly out of gratitude to the government which granted him asylum during World War II. Apart from the top-class works of European art ranging from Gothic to Impressionist, the museum also displays French furniture, wall hangings, tableware, and art nouveau jewellery by René Lalique, and has a further section devoted to Far Eastern and Islamic pottery and textiles.

Exhibit in the Museu Calouste Gulbenkian

★★ **Museu do Azulejo**, Rua da Madre de Deus 4, tel: 814 7747 (Tuesday to Sunday 10am–2pm) documents the development of tile design. It is housed in the Madre de Deus monastery which was founded in 1507 by Leonor, the pious sister of King Manuel. The **Lisbon Panorama** shows how Lisbon looked before the earthquake.

Museu do Azulejo exhibit

★ **Palácio dos Marquesas da Fronteira**, Largo de São Domingos de Benfica 1 (conducted tours only, Monday to Saturday 10.30am–noon), is situated near the Sete-Rios Zoo on the northern edge of the Parque Florestal de Monsanto. This palace and famous garden has remained in the hands of the same family ever since it was built in the 17th century. The ★★★ **gardens** represent the embodiment of Portuguese garden design: a geometric box tree terrace with statues and fountains; a pond (*tanque*) and summer house covered with cobalt blue *azulejos*; a shady corner with exotic trees, cool grottoes, niches and low walls, all decorated with more *azulejos*.

Route 2

Costa do Sol – Serra de Sintra – Mafra

As this route includes a number of detours, a car is preferable. Without a vehicle, a shortened day trip is possible but Mafra would have to be missed out. In this case catch the suburban train to Cascais from Cais do Sodré station, then take the bus from Cascais to Sintra via Colares. Trains return to Rossío station from Sintra. For information about organised coach tours, consult a travel agent in Lisbon.

Estoril beach

Sheltered from the Atlantic winds and enjoying a mild climate, the Costa do Sol with its main resorts of Estoril and Cascais became known in the 19th century as the Portuguese Riviera. Once the haunt of exiled kings and the international jet set, it is now a fairly prosperous suburb of Lisbon. The 35-km (22-mile) coast road (Estrada Marginal) to Cascais is very busy and is bordered by villas, both old and new, satellite developments, building sites,

parks, historic fortresses and agricultural land. During summer weekends, day-trippers pour out of Lisbon and make for the beaches along this section of coast, even though the quality of the water here leaves much to be desired. Nevertheless, the region has retained much of its charm. Cascais and Estoril both have good rail links and so are ideal as bases from which to explore Lisbon and its environs.

Elegance at Estoril

The grand villas and hotels of **Estoril** testify to the international appeal that the resort once enjoyed. The famous **Palácio Hotel** became the home of King Umberto of Italy when he was deposed and it was also used as a centre for espionage during World War II. German and Allied secret agents are said to have met for discussions at the bar here and Jewish refugees, for whom neutral Portugal was the final staging post before fleeing to America, were obliged to pay their hotel bill by handing over family treasures.

Estoril still has an exclusive feel and the influence of British expatriates is very much in evidence. There is a

The harbour at Cascais

casino at the head of palm-lined gardens and one of Portugal's best golf courses (Clube de Golf do Estoril) is situated nearby. A new golf course (Penha Longa) has recently opened at the foot of the Serra de Sintra under Japanese management.

Despite the rapid growth of the town, **Cascais** remains a fishing port and colourful boats still set out from the small harbour. Their catch is auctioned every day on the **Lota**. This busy town, the main tourist resort on the Costa do Sol has an attractive old quarter with an animated pedestrian zone, and many cafés and restaurants, although they are rather expensive. The narrow beach extends as far as Estoril. Take a stroll through the quiet old town, by the citadel and the carefully maintained municipal park (Parque do Marechal Carmona). On the coastal side of the park stands the residence of a Portuguese aristocrat that dates from the turn of the century. It is now the **Museu Conde de Castro Guimarães** (11am–1pm, 2.30–5pm, closed Monday and public holidays) and has displays of prehistoric finds, gold and silver work and Portuguese furniture.

The Cascais Music Festival (classical and jazz) is held in July and August.

Fishermen put to sea

Cabo da Roca

The road out of Cascais to the north follows the increasingly rocky coast towards the broad and exposed dunes at ★ **Guincho**. This section of coast is a haven not just for surfers and windsurfers, but also for the less energetic gourmet as it boasts a fine a selection of fine fish restaurants, for example, **Mestre Zé**.

On the return journey to Colares and Sintra, there are a number of detours which are worth exploring. The steep cliffs at ★ **Cabo da Roca** near **Azoia** mark the westernmost point on the European mainland. Branch off in Azoia for ★ **Peninha** where the view from a windswept point extends over the Costa do Sol as far as Lisbon. The beach at **Praia das Maças** is a particular favourite with Lisbon families. Other popular beaches include those at **Praia Grande**, **Azenhas** and **Praia da Aguda**. The cafés in the village square at **Colares** can provide welcome refreshment. The road from Colares passes some grand *quintas* with **Quinta da Monserrate** (*see below*) among the most interesting. The **Palácio da Seteais** was built in the 18th century for a Dutch diamond trader.

Even though the summer sun may be shining all over Portugal, a bank of cloud will probably shroud this small mountain region by the coast. In high summer the ★★ **Serra da Sintra** is considerably cooler than Lisbon and over the centuries it has become popular with wealthy city dwellers. Two royal palaces and countless country mansions built by the nobility bear witness to that. The moist microclimate creates the ideal soil conditions for an abundance of vegetation and English poets such as Lord Byron have expressed their love of the countryside around Sintra. For him it was a 'glorious Eden'. When, in the 19th century, landscape gardening became a fashionable pursuit for the wealthy middle classes, a number of amateur botanists sought fame by designing exotic parks and gardens. Sir Francis Cook, an English textile tycoon, was responsible for the gardens at Monserrate. The German Ferdinand of Saxe-Coburg laid out the Parque da Pena and also transformed large areas of the stony Serra by planting trees.

Town houses in Sintra

The old Moorish town of ★ **Sintra** was conquered in 1147 by Alfonso Henriques, but it was some years later before Portuguese kings and noblemen discovered the benefits of the cool hillsides in summer. Apart from the palaces, which are obviously the highlights of the town from the coach tour operators' point of view, it is also pleasant to take a stroll along the lanes and winding paths of Sintra. Delightful *quintas* overgrown with camellias and pale roses lie in the quiet shade of palms and cedars.

Paço Real and its conical towers

From the 14th century to the beginning of the 20th century the ★ **Paço Real** (conducted tours 10am–12.30pm, 2–4.30pm, closed Wednesday and public holidays) was the summer residence of the Portuguese royal family. The building, a mixture of various styles, is crowned by the two conical towers of the palace kitchens which have now become a distinctive symbol for the town of Sintra. Moorish traditions are still in evidence with rooms arranged in a haphazard way around small shaded courtyards. Walls in many of the rooms are covered with fine *azulejos*. Those in the ★★ **Hall of Arabs** were manufactured in Seville in the 15th and 16th centuries and they are said to be the finest collection on the Iberian peninsula.

Azulejos in the Paço Real

Moorish traditions can also be seen in the wooden ceilings which cover the rooms like the lid of a chest. The Mudéjar ceiling in the **Chapel** is particularly striking. Note also the beautifully tiled floor here, said to date from the 15th century. Most of the rooms included in the conducted tour were built during the reign of Manuel I who much preferred to spend his time in Sintra as Lisbon was badly affected by plagues. Apart from the *azulejo* frescoes and the painted timber ceilings, many of the furnishings are simple. Lavishly decorated wall hangings, carpets and cushions gave the rooms colour and warmth. As late as the 18th century, the royal family and courtiers still preferred floor cushions in Arab style to chairs. The turreted wall of the old Moorish castle, the **Castelo dos Mouros**, can be seen from the entrance to the palace. It winds along the crest of the hill like a miniature Great Wall of China. Ask at the *turismo* for directions to the castle.

Palácio da Pena

The pseudo-medieval ★ **Palácio da Pena** (10am–1pm, 2–5pm, closed Monday and public holidays) looks down on Sintra from the highest peak. It is often called the 'Portuguese Neuschwanstein' after the fairy-tale castle in southern Germany. The steep hill, castle and garden, which cover an area of 270ha (666 acres) provide an early example of the way 19th-century designers sought to combine architecture and landscape to create a harmonious and romantic setting.

Work on the royal summer residence started in 1840 on the site of an abandoned Manueline monastery. The work was commissioned by a German prince, Ferdinand of Saxe-Coburg, who invested huge sums of money in the project right up to his death in 1885. The interior can be visited and the rooms remain as they were left when Queen Amelia fled to England in 1910 when Portugal became a republic. The monastery **cloisters** and **chapel** with a splendid marble ★ **altar** by Nicolas de Chanterène (*see page 85*) were incorporated into the structure.

The huge ★ **park** which stretches over the hills also required the expenditure of considerable energy and resources. Features include a rose garden, tropical ferns and lakes, exotic summer houses and a wood with Japanese fir trees and Chinese yews.

Monserrate park and castle

★ **Monserrate** (daily 10am–5pm), situated 3km (2 miles) outside Sintra, is probably the most famous park in the area. In the 1860s the English millionaire Sir Francis Cook set about creating a fabulous garden alongside a Moorish-Gothic-Indian fairy-tale castle. Exotic giant trees, 25 varieties of palms, camellias and tree ferns are among the 3,000 species originally planted here that still thrive in the unique, greenhouse-like microclimate. The Australian tree ferns which Cook himself imported are naturalised in the Serra.

Halfway between Sintra and Lisbon by the new highway lies the royal summer palace of ★ **Queluz** (10am–1pm, 2–5pm, closed Tuesday). This bright salmon-pink mansion was built in 1747 in rococo style. The ★ **gardens**, designed by the Frenchman Jean Baptiste Robillon, consist of wide box tree terraces, statues and fountains and they are probably more interesting than the interior. They are reputed to have been the setting for some notorious summer night festivals. Young noblemen would have used the canal which runs through the lower section of the garden to take their lady companions for a row. Rococo *azulejos* adorn the canal basin.

Noites de Queluz is a summer music festival in which performers wear traditional costumes – for further information enquire at the *turismo* in Sintra or Lisbon.

Queluz Summer Palace

Magnificent Mafra

★ **Mafra** is situated some 20km (12 miles) north of Sintra by the N9. Buses leave from Sintra station and from Praça Marquês de Pombal in Lisbon. The **monastery-palace** at Mafra (conducted tours 10am–1pm, 2–5pm, closed Tuesday), built between 1707 and 1750, was a major project planned by João V. Intended as a thanksgiving for the birth of an heir, it was to be on such a grand scale that it would even eclipse Spain's El Escorial. Over 50,000 men were press-ganged into working on the scheme and then gagged by the soldiers who guarded them. The full story is told in the novel *The Memorial* by the Portuguese writer José Saramagos. Funds for the building came from the sale of Brazilian gold and diamonds. The main facade is 220m (720ft) long and behind it are 880 rooms, some of which have had very little use.

The marble **basilica** which was consecrated in 1730 is as big as a cathedral. Workshops at the site were used to train a whole generation of Portuguese master craftsmen under the direction of the German architect Johann Friedrich Ludwig and other specialists from elsewhere in Europe. Both Machado de Castro, Portugal's greatest baroque sculptor, and Mateus Vicente, the architect of the Estrêla church in Lisbon, worked on the palace at Mafra. The majestic structure is of a symmetrical design with the basilica as the centrepiece. The proportions of the building are accentuated by the domes on the flanking pavilions and the twin towers and dome of the basilica. The palace was once home to 300 monks and the pharmacy, hospital, dormitory and kitchen are particularly interesting. The ★ **library** houses 30,000 volumes, the most celebrated being the first edition of Camões' *Lusiads*.

There is no need to go too far for refreshment after the two-hour tour. Directly opposite the palace stands the inviting **Pastelaria Dom João V**. Souvenir shops sell a wide range of locally-produced pottery.

The hospital and library books

The park in Caldas da Rainha

Route 3

Lisbon – Óbidos – Alcobaça – Batalha – Fátima – Tomar – Lisbon (345km/215 miles) *See map pages 30–1*

This round trip covers all the main sites of architectural interest dating from the Middle Ages and the Manueline period. Travel agents in Lisbon organise coach tours that follow a similar itinerary.

Take the A1 motorway from Lisbon as far as Vila Franca de Xira and then follow the N1 to Caldas da Rainha. Alternatively, this route could start with visits to Sintra and Mafra (*see pages 33–5*) and then continue northwards on the N8 with detours to the resorts along the coast and the rocky Peniche peninsula.

Cabbage leaf pottery

Caldas da Rainha is a spa with sulphur springs where, at the end of the 15th century, King Manuel's sister Léonor found a cure for her rheumatism. Unusual souvenirs on sale here include plates in a cabbage leaf design.

Óbidos

From Caldas da Rainha, follow the N8 through hilly terrain as far as ★★ **Óbidos**, just a few miles further south. The town is now under a preservation order and in high season tourists arrive by coach to admire the white houses decked with flowers. Despite the commercialisation, this picturesque old town enclosed by a ring of battlemented walls is well worth a visit. Even in 1282 when it was visited by King Dinis, his young wife Isabella fell in love with the place, whereupon the king made her a gift of it. Later Portuguese kings repeated the gesture.

After parking in one of the car parks outside, enter the town through a gate in the wall. **Rua Direita**, lined with souvenir shops, is the main street linking one gate with the

Praça de Santa Maria. The parish church of **Santa Maria** dates from the 16th century and contains 17th-century *azulejos* and the ★ **Renaissance tomb** of J. de Noronha. At the end of this street stands the old fortress which has been converted into a *pousada*. Steps lead up on to the wall and it is then possible to make a full circuit of the town. The walk offers fine views over both the town and the surrounding countryside. There are a number of inviting restaurants in the town, often in historic houses, but if they look to be too crowded, then the **Dom João V** outside the walls near the large baroque **Senhor da Pedra** church is a good alternative.

Azulejos in Santa Maria

Return to Caldas da Rainha and follow the N8 northwards. Branch off to the attractive holiday resort of **São Martinho do Porto** and then continue up the coast to **Nazaré**. The stretch of coast between **Peniche** and **Figuera da Foz** is more or less one long beach. Nazaré, the main resort along this section of coast, was once a busy fishing harbour and the fishermen here are said to be ancestors of the Phoenicians, but in recent years the fishing families have been overwhelmed by tourists. A new harbour has been built and the boats no longer have to be pulled on to the beach with oxen, as the old postcards show. The beach is now lined with rows of brightly coloured bathing tents overlooked from the promenade behind by restaurants and tourist shops. A funicular railway links the town with the suburb of **Sítio** on the clifftops some 110m (360ft) above.

Nazaré beach

Some 11km/7 miles inland the huge medieval Cistercian monastery at ★★★ **Alcobaça** guards the tombs of the Burgundian dynasty, Portugal's first royal house, and ranks as one of the country's most important monuments. The monastery lies at the heart of a large fertile agricultural region which has been tended by monks for many centuries. It owes its existence to King Alfonso Henriques who granted the land to the Cistercian order after the defeat of the Moors at Santarém in 1147. The king was indebted to the Cistercians, not just because they had supported his military campaign, but because a leading member of the order, Bernard of Clairvaux, had negotiated with the pope and his Castilian neighbours for the recognition of an independent Portuguese kingdom. The monastery which was completed in 1222 grew to be one of the wealthiest and most important in the whole of Europe. According to the rules of the Cistercian order, only 999 – 'one less than a thousand' – monks were allowed to reside there. Until the 18th century Alcobaça was the spiritual centre of the country, but earthquake damage and repeated looting by the French in the 19th century resulted in the burning of the altars.

Alcobaça Monastery

In 1930 it was decided to restore the abbey as a national monument and it is now protected by a preservation order. The front of the monastery complex extends for 220m (720ft) with the 18th-century baroque facade of the Gothic monastery church at its centre. The early Gothic ★★ **interior** is unusual not just for its dimensions (106m/348ft long, 20m/65ft high and only 17m/56ft wide). The three aisles of equal height separated by two lines of 12 narrow bays with Gothic vaulting also combine to create one of the finest examples of the ascetic beauty and majesty of plain French Cistercian architecture. The effect is even more stark as the old furnishings are lost. Only the fine Gothic ★★ **sarcophagi** of Inês de Castro and King Pedro I – at either end of the transept – remain. The couple in Portugal's most famous love story were entombed facing each other on the wishes of Pedro so that 'upon their resurrection they would see each other first'.

Tomb of King Pedro

The poet Camões recounted the story of Pedro's love for Inês in his *Lusiads*. The affair began in 1328 when Crown Prince Pedro found he did not love Constança of Castille, the bride chosen for him, but preferred Inês, one of the ladies of the court. Their love was mutual and so, when Constança died prematurely, the prince publicly confirmed his liaison with Inês and she bore him two sons. Pedro's father, Alfonso IV, however, was unhappy about the relationship as he feared possible Castilian claims to the Portuguese throne. Inês and her two children were stabbed to death at their country home, now known as the Quinta das Lagrimas, the 'villa of tears', near Coimbra (*see page* 57). Alfonso died two years later and Pedro sought to avenge her death. The murderers were found and their hearts ripped from their bodies while they were still alive. The body of Inês was exhumed, dressed in regal clothes, placed on a throne in Coimbra cathedral and the country's dignitaries were obliged to kiss her hand. Her body was then carried in a torch-light procession to Alcobaça.

The cloister at Alcobaça

The ★ **cloister** is probably the most impressive section of the monastic buildings. The lower level is 13th-century, while the upper level in Manueline style was started at the beginning of the 16th century. On the north side stands a Gothic **fountain house** in front of the **refectory**. Note the early Gothic **reading desk**. To the right is the ★ **kitchen** with a huge chimney breast. William Beckford, who visited here in 1794, spoke of the most 'extraordinary feeding temple' that he had ever seen, where exotic delicacies such as shark fin and swallows' nest were prepared.

For a little bodily fortification after the visit try an *açorda de marisco* (fish soup) in the popular **Trindade** restaurant in **Praça D. Alfonso Henriques**.

Aljubarrota, 6km (4 miles) further north, was the scene of a great battle with Spain in 1385. Victory assured Portugal of independence from its much bigger neighbour for another two centuries. In recognition of the military achievements work started in 1388 on a grand religious monument, the monastery of **Santa Maria da Vitória** in ★★★ **Batalha** (= battle), not far from the site of the conflict. The abbey here is also the last resting place of some members of the Avis dynasty, which was founded by the victor of the Battle of Aljubarrota, João I, an illegitimate son of Pedro I. His body lies in the Founder's Chapel (1435) together with his English wife, Philippa of Lancaster and their children. Henry the Navigator is also buried here. The work on the abbey was not completed until 1533 and so it displays a variety of architectural styles ranging from French and English Gothic to Manueline. Nevertheless, great beauty and originality can be seen in some of the features: the high, elegant walls of the church ★ **interior** (88m/288ft long and 32m/105ft wide); the superb star-shaped cupola above the ★ **Founder's Chapel**; the ★★★ **cloister** (Claustro Real) with the richly decorated arcades and the enchanting fountain house; the ★★ **chapterhouse** with its bold, unsupported vaulting that has withstood all earthquakes; and the Manueline ★★★ **Capelas Imparfeitas**, designed as a royal mausoleum. The massive buttresses around the inside of the octagon were intended to support a dome which was never finished.

Batalha Monastery

Apse and star-shaped cupola above the Founder's Chapel

The journey on to Tomar can be broken by a detour to **Mira de Aire** where caves, the biggest in Portugal, are linked together by artificial tunnels.

Fátima is one of the most famous places of pilgrimage in Europe, but it is more a monument to a belief in miracles than to art. It was here on 13 May 1917 and on the 13th day of each subsequent month until October of the same year that the Virgin Mary is said to have appeared before three peasant children. The church which was built in 1928 stands at the end of a square twice as large as St Peter's Square in Rome. Motorists can expect traffic jams on the anniversaries of the apparitions.

The small town of ★ **Tomar** on the banks of the **Rio Nabão** lies 32km (20 miles) away along the N113. The ★★★ **Convent of the Knights of Christ** dominates this pleasant old town with its park and a river. In 1160 the Knights Templar founded a castle here and it played an important part in the great victory over the Moors at Santarém. It later stood guard over the newly-won territory by the Tagus. The Order of Knights Templar was dissolved in 1314 and King Dinis created the Order of the Knights of Christ for the purpose of 'defending the faith, fighting the Moors and expanding the influence of the Portuguese monarchy'. The difference between the two bodies was that the king controlled the new order. The Grand Master was always the king himself or one of the princes – both Henry the Navigator and King Manuel held the post.

The duties of the Order of Knights became more important when the Voyages of Discovery extended Portuguese interests worldwide, as the knights administered the new provinces. The large tracts of land which they owned and the commission that they earned from their responsibilities in the colonies transformed the order into the richest in Christendom. The red cross of the Knights of Christ was an emblem for the Manueline period and it always adorned the sails of the Portuguese caravels.

At the heart of the complex stands the dignified ★★ **Rotunda**. Built in 1160 the Byzantine features bear witness to the Crusader years. The church with its ★ **high choir** and ★ **chapterhouse** was added by Manuel I. The ★★ **west facade** of the choir is famous for an extraordinary Manueline window. Seaweed, anchor chains, mussels, cork, twisted cables and other motifs associated with the sea are wrapped around two convoluted masts. These are then crowned with the Portuguese coat-of-arms, armillary spheres and, above it all, the cross of the Order of the Knights of Christ. As with all masterpieces from the Manueline period, the names of Boytac, Castilho and Arruda feature prominently.

Convent of the Knights of Christ: the famous Manueline window

Under João I, the knights' order was transformed into a monks' order and a new monastery was built. The pure harmony of the ★★ **Dos Filipes cloister** has no equal on the Iberian peninsula.

Return to Lisbon via **Encontramento** and the motorway or link in with Route 2 or Route 4.

The Dos Felipes cloister

Route 4

Alentejo and the Algarve

The wide expanse of the Alentejo is the most thinly populated area of Portugal. Since Roman times it has been the Portuguese granary. Despite difficulties with irrigation, cereals, cork oaks, vines and olives have flourished here. Little towns on hilltops gleam white in the bright sun while, in the countryside, large landowners inhabit isolated *montes* or large farmhouses. During the Carnation Revolution thousands of landowners were dispossessed and communist agricultural collectives were founded, but people still hope that change will come. The situation is almost back to what it was and the unemployment level is higher here than anywhere else in Portugal.

Taking the slow lane

The contrast between the interior and the small coastal Algarve province could not be more marked. The Algarve is Portugal's holiday playground. Two-thirds of all tourists make for here and the development of this beautiful stretch of coast has proceeded at an alarming rate.

The name is Arabic. Al-Gharb, 'the west', was how the Moors described this region which they dominated for 500 years. The 200-km (125-mile) strip of coast is divided into the Barlavento, the rocky Algarve west of Faro, and the flat Sotavento, the sandy Algarve in the east.

Route 4 is broken up into two stages so that it can start either from Lisbon or Faro.

4A: Lisbon – Serra da Arrabida – Setúbal – Sines – Sagres – Lagos – Faro (490km/305 miles)

This stage leads first of all to the Setúbal peninsula and then follows the Alentejan Atlantic coast, the Costa Azul (the Blue Coast). The charm of the coast here lies in the alternating sandy beaches and rocky cliffs and happily it has not yet been disfigured by blocks of hotels and apartments. The main bastions of tourism on the Algarve coast are to be found between Sagres and Faro.

Leave Lisbon on the Ponte 25 de Abril. At the turning to **Almada** a fast road branches off to the west to the **Costa da Caparica**, a 20-km (12-mile) long beach favoured by the *lisboetes*. About 11km (7 miles) after the bridge, leave the motorway and follow the N378 to Santana. A little further on lies **Sesimbra**, a fishing village that is being increasingly overwhelmed by new hotels for the burgeoning tourist industry. The lonely, rocky headland at **Cabo Espichel**, on the western tip of the Setúbal peninsula, is worth a visit for the fine ★★ **view**. Follow the N379 out of Santana as far as **Aldeia dos Irmãos** where the N379-1 leads down through the thickly wooded slopes of the ★ **Serra da Arrabida**. Looking down at the shimmering blue ocean it would be easy to imagine that these tranquil waters were the Mediterranean. The range of hills above is designated as a nature reserve, in part closed off to the public to protect the extraordinary flora.

Bay in Serra da Arrabida

Behind the Serra da Arrabida, the N379 crosses the Azeitão, where the sweet grapes for Setúbal's muscatel are cultivated. One of Portugal's finest wines matures in the **Fonseca** cellars, situated in the centre of **Vila Nogueira de Azeitão** (Monday to Friday 9am–noon, 2–5pm). Nearby two interesting summer palaces were built by the aristocracy in the 16th century. Set in a park is the attractive ★ **Quinta das Torres**, a hotel with a splendid restaurant where diners can sit and admire the Italian Renaissance *azulejos* on the wall. In the neighbouring town of **Vila Fresca de Azeitão**, to the left of the N10 opposite the bus station, stands the ★★ **Quinta da Bacalhoa** (Monday to Saturday 1–5pm) and here too there are some unusual *azulejo* decorations to inspect. The *quinta*, with its exotic domes, is privately owned but the ★ **gardens** may be visited. Of the fine 16th-century ★ **azulejos** in the garden casino, some display Islamic-style geometric patterns, others are illustrated in Italian Renaissance style.

Igreja de Jesus

The N10 passes through hilly terrain to **Setúbal**, Portugal's third-biggest town (pop. 100,000). It is a port and industrial centre, but the traditional industries such as fish processing and shipbuilding have been undergoing a period of uncertainty. The old town centre on the hillside is an interesting place for a stroll. The ★ **Igreja de Jesus** (Church of Jesus) at the north end of the Avenida 22 de Dezembro is the oldest building in the town and dates from the end of the 15th century. Manueline features here include the twisted pillars supporting the vaulting and the spiral ribs of the vault above the chancel. The **Museu de Cidade** (9am–12.30pm, 2–5.30pm, closed Monday and public holidays) in the adjoining monastery cloisters contains an altar table c. 1500 from the Church of Jesus.

A ferry plies between Setúbal and the long, sandy **Tróia** peninsula where one of the country's biggest holiday complexes is situated. A little further on by the N253-1 lie the scanty remains of **Cetóbriga**. At Comporta the N253 branches off to Alcácer do Sal. The road runs alongside the **Rio Sado Delta**, a nature reserve and the habitat for some rare bird species. Salt is collected from the marshes and the area is also used for the cultivation of rice. The fields lie below sea-level and a series of canals and sluice gates control the water flow.

Alcácer do Sal still has its lookouts

★ **Alcácer do Sal**, or the 'Castle of Salt' dominates the Sado Valley. The fortress was in Moorish hands from the 8th century until 1217 when it was captured by the Christians. The monopoly in salt and the production of cereals on the Alentejan plain guaranteed prosperity from the Middle Ages onwards. The castle and the small Romanesque **Santa Maria** church (12th- to 13th-century) overlook the attractive old town.

Cork oak in Grândola

The N120 passes through the pine forests of the Sado Valley and on to **Grândola**. This town, a centre of cork production, became famous through a protest song that was banned during the Salazar years. Entitled *Grândola –Vila Morena* (Grândola – Brown Town), it signalled the start of the Carnation Revolution when broadcast on the radio. The main highway to Sines bypasses Grândola. A twisting, but more picturesque route is the old country road via **Santa Margarida da Serra** to **Santiago do Cacém** with its well-preserved baroque townhouses. The ruins of a Knights Templar castle dominate the town and there is a fine view from here towards the coast. Some 2km (1¼ miles) away lies the excavated Celtic-Roman settlement of ★ **Miróbriga** (Tuesday to Sunday 9am–noon, 1.30–5pm). The ★ **Museu Regional** documents the history of cork manufacture and everyday life in the region.

Sines lies at the end of a fast road lined by huge oil refineries. During the 1970s a large deep-water harbour for oil tankers was constructed here and the petrochemical industry has now become well established. The old town lies on the clifftops above the old fishing harbour. In 1460 Vasco da Gama, the first European to sail to India, was born here. The sandy beaches at Sines are spoilt by the port installations nearby, but the resorts of **Praia de Galé**, **Melides** and **Santo André** to the north and **Porto Covo** and **Vila Nova de Milfontes** to the south are gaining in popularity.

Praia de Galé

Cabo de São Vincente

Ponte da Piedade

The N120 continues southward through the old towns of **Odemira** and **Aljezur** to **Vila do Bispo**, where pleasant cafés surround the main square. Here the N268 branches off to ★ **Sagres**. It was here that Henry the Navigator established his school of seamanship. All that remains is a small chapel and a gigantic *rosa dos ventos* or 'compass card' carved out of the stone. Further west is the windblown ★★ **Cabo de São Vicente** or Cape of St Vincent. The breathtaking views from the 60-m (200-ft) high clifftop draw many visitors to this rocky promontory, the southwest corner of the European mainland.

The Atlantic coast between Sagres and Lagos is gradually attracting tourist investment, but there are no modern hotel blocks here yet. Narrow lanes lead down from the N125 to the beaches which remain quiet and unspoilt.

The ancient port of ★ **Lagos** was once an important centre on this section of coast, primarily because it served as the main trading post for slaves from Africa. In 1443 under the arcades of the **Casa da Alfândega** by the Praça da Republica, the first slave auction was held. The first Voyages of Discovery left from here and also the suicidal campaign to Morocco led by King Sebastião (*see page 85*). While the extensive fortress wall succumbed to the violent earthquake of 1755, the baroque 17th-century church of ★ **Santo António** survived. Inside are some extraordinarily beautiful examples of *talha dourada*.

The beaches at ★ **Meia Praia**, ★ **Praia Dona Ana** and ★★ **Ponte da Piedade** have become very popular.

Leave Lagos on the N125. The **Bravura** reservoir is used by watersports enthusiasts and can be reached by taking a turning in **Odiáxere** along the N125-9 a journey which winds through pretty countryside. Some 9km (5 miles) after Odiáxere a road off to the right leads down to three fine beaches, the ★ **Montes de Alvor**, ★ **Alvor** and ★ **Praia dos Três Irmãos**. Some distance behind the steep cliffs that overlook the beaches stand a number of exclusive hotels and holiday homes.

The next major town on the N125 is **Portimão**, an industrial centre and port at the mouth of the **Rio Arade** and the second most important town on the Algarve coast. The section of coast between Faro and Portimão is devoted almost entirely to mass tourism. About 2km (1¼ miles) to the east lies the beautiful **Praia da Rocha** beach which is dominated by some bizarre rock formations.

Sunflowers in Serra de Monchique

The ★ **Serra de Monchique**, lying some 25km (16 miles) inland from Portimão, is a region famous for its lush and varied vegetation. It is a green oasis of fruit orchards, grazing meadows and woodland. There is a small medicinal spring at **Caldas de Monchique** (only open in summer) which lies 7km (4 miles) south of **Monchique**. This picturesque hillside town and regional centre (445m/1,460ft above sea level) is noted for its fine *medronho*, a brandy distilled from the fruit of the strawberry tree. The highest peak of the Serra, the **Foia** (902m/2,960ft), is to be found 8km (5 miles) to the west.

On the return journey, a visit to the sleepy town of ★ **Silves** is thoroughly recommended. In its earlier years it was known as **Xelb** and was the capital of the Moorish Al-Gharb province. The **castle complex** in red sandstone is a reminder of Moorish dominance between the 8th and 13th centuries and the new **museum** is the first museum in Portugal to document Arabic influences. The Gothic **cathedral** was built in the 13th century by the Portuguese. The N124-1 connects Silves with the main coast road at

Silves Castle – built by the Moors and conquered by the Portuguese

Soaking up the sun at Albufeira

The picturesque side of Faro

Lagoa. During the summer this busy route (N125) is often badly congested. Many of the tiny fishing villages between here and Faro have grown into major resorts. The coastline between **Carvoeira** and **Armação de Pêra** has several sandy bays – no longer so quiet but still very beautiful. The sandy beach at Armação de Pêra extends for 6km (4 miles) towards Albufeira, but the spread of concrete hotels and apartment blocks has continued unabated along this stretch of coastline.

Albufeira likes to call itself the Saint-Tropez of the Algarve. Bars, souvenir shops, boutiques and discos abound. The heart of the old fishing village has retained much of its charm, but the beach is crowded in summer. **Praia da Falésia**, 8km/5 miles further east, is a good alternative.

Vilamoura is the next tourist centre. Its development has been aided by the construction of a huge marina and a golf course. **Quarteira** follows a few miles further on, but this modern resort, a sprawl of tower blocks, has little to commend it. **Vale do Lobo** to the southeast is a luxury resort largely populated by the British. There are two golf courses here and another at **Quinta do Lago**. The latter is said by many golfers to be the finest course in Portugal.

Faro (pop. 42,000) is the Algarve's administrative centre. The closest most visitors get to the town centre is the busy airport but, behind the old town walls and the chaotic suburban roads, an attractive old town has been preserved. The Gothic **Cathedral**, however, suffered badly in the Great Eartquake of 1755. The interior is predominantly Renaissance. Many visitors to the Algarve resorts come to Faro for shopping and **Rua de Santo António** is a popular pedestrian precinct. The **Museu Arqueológico** (Tuesday to Sunday 10am–noon, 2–5pm) has interesting displays and the **Museu Marítimo** (Monday to Friday 9.30am–12.30pm, 2–5.30pm) documents the history of the fishing industry on the Algarve. The **Largo do Carmo** church on the square of the same name houses a macabre ossuary. To the east of the town the **Ria Formosa** nature reserve surrounds an extensive lagoon. It is an important staging post for many species of migratory birds. Boat trips leave from **Cais da Porta Nova**.

4B: Faro – Vila Real de Santo António – Mértola – Beja – Serpa – Moura – Évora (420km/260 miles)

Take the N2 out of Faro for about 9km (5 miles) as far as the turning to **Estói**. One of the few large *quintas* of southern Portugal is situated here. It dates from the 18th century, was renovated around 1900 but is now in a state of decay. The ★ **gardens** are filled with statues, *azulejos* and Roman mosaics from the excavations at **Milreu**.

Take the N2-6 back to the coast at **Olhão** (pop. 15,000).

The town is a port and not a particularly inviting place for a long stay as there is a pervading smell of fish. The **fishing quarter** is interesting, however, as its houses are cube-shaped casbah-style with terraces and openwork chimneys. These north African-style dwellings are not relics from Moorish times but were built during the 19th century. Take a stroll around the busy fish market and visit one of the many fish restaurants. During high season, ferries ply regularly from Olhão harbour across to the sandy offshore islands.

The N125 leads east through fields of almond and carob trees to ★ **Tavira.** This sleepy town with pretty, pastel-coloured houses and historic buildings lost its *raison d'être* when the harbour silted up, but happily it has not been spoilt by tourism. The settlement straddles the tranquil **Rio Gilão** and the two sides of the town are linked by a bridge that dates from Roman times. There is a fish market near the harbour and in the nearby streets a number of small restaurants serve fresh tuna. A long, narrow sandy island, the **Ilha de Tavira**, stands between the town and the open sea. The best beaches are to be found here and in summer a ferry shuttles across to **Quatro Aguas**.

The border town of **Vila Real de Santo António** (pop. 13,500) is a further 23km (14 miles) along the N125. The road passes a number of holiday villages such as **Cabanas** and **Manta Rota** which have sprung up in recent years by the fine sandy beaches. Vila Real on the **Rio Guadiana** earns its living from fish processing and the border traffic with Spain. Badly damaged by the Great Earthquake of 1755, the town centre was re-designed by Pombal in a rectangular plan based around the main square. Now that a new bridge into Spain has been built (completed in 1991), the town centre has seen a reduction in passing trade, but the nearby resort of **Monte Gordo** with its miles of sandy beaches is becoming very popular.

The N122 leads northwards out of Vila Real through the delightful upland landscape of the eastern Algarve. Walks into the thinly populated mountains or along the Rio Guadiana Valley can be very rewarding but there are still no waymarkings. The main centres include **Alcoutim**, **Foz de Odeleite** or **Almada de Ouro**. River trips to Alcoutim leave from the harbour in Vila Real.

Castro Marim with its 14th-century Knights of Christ castle is surrounded by salt marshes. The **Sapal de Castro Marim** wetland nature reserve between the town and Vila Real provides a habitat for a number of wading birds such as herons and storks. Flamingoes often use these marshes as a staging post too.

The N122 winds its way northwards through unspoilt hilly terrain along the Guadiana. The village of ★ **Mértola**

Sleepy Tavira

Vila Real de Santo Antonio

A strategic base for storks

(70km/43 miles) is worth stopping to admire. The pretty white houses occupy a commanding location on terraces beneath a ruined castle, once the site of Roman fortifications, and there is a magnificent ★ **view** from the hilltop. The village ★ **church**, once a Moorish mosque, has four naves, some interesting late Romanesque and Islamic capitals and a *mihrab*, an Islamic prayer niche.

Mértola church

The next stop on the N122 is **Beja**. This is the second-biggest town in the Alentejo and stands in a broad plain used mainly for the cultivation of wheat. Beja was known in Roman times as Pax Julia and it was an important centre in Lusitania. The castle and tall keep go back to Roman times. Visigoths later established a bishopric here. An interesting collection of *azulejos* comprises one section of the ★ **Museu Regional** in the old Gothic-Manueline **da Conceição** monastery. The small **Santo Amaro** church dates from Visigothic times. A **museum** here documents aspects of the Visigothic period.

Moura castle, a place of legend

Some 29km (18 miles) to the east along the N260 lies ★ **Serpa**, a typical whitewashed Alentejan town where time seems to have stood still. Despite the picturesque backdrop of **town walls**, the Gothic **Santa Maria** and **Santo António** churches and the ruined castle on the hilltop, this remote little town remains poor.

About 40km (25 miles) north of Serpa on the N255 lies ★ **Moura**. Its name reveals its Moorish past and a famous legend, if it is to be believed, gives some idea of the town's violent history. The Moorish princess Salúquia is said to have thrown herself from the castle tower on the morning of her wedding when she heard of her bridegroom's death at the hands of Christians. Well worth seeking out are the Gothic-Manueline **church**, the Renaissance cloister at the **Carmo monastery** and the old Moorish quarter, known as **Mouraria**. Low houses line the narrow streets, sometimes ornamented with *azulejos*.

The N386/385 wind their way northward to **Mourão** on the N256, the road that comes in from the Spanish border and then heads northwest to Évora. Just across the Rio Guadiana along a lonely side road stands ★ **Monsaraz**, the old border fortress of the Knights Templar. High above the Guadiana plain, this picture-book town with old, whitewashed houses and a breathtaking panoramic view makes an ideal spot for an overnight stay. It has restaurants and a few small pensions (**Dom Nuno** is recommended). There is also an *estalagem* (hotel) beneath the castle.

Veteran of the times in Monsaraz

The road from Monsaraz rejoins the N256 just outside **Reguengos de Monsaraz** and ★★★ **Évora** (pop. 45,000) is 36km (22 miles) further on. This is the largest and finest town in the Alentejo region and in 1986 it was awarded international heritage status by UNESCO. But it ought not

to be thought that Évora is some sort of museum town – it is a very lively centre, although it is a shame that the tidal wave of cars entering the old town has not yet been stemmed. There is a car park outside the town walls.

Évora Cathedral cloisters
Ruins of the royal palace

Romans, Moors and medieval Portuguese kings have left their mark on the town. In the 16th century, a local interpretation of Renaissance style found expression here. It will take at least a day to visit and fully appreciate the more than 30 churches, monasteries and Moorish-style palaces in Évora.

The best place to start the tour is the central ★ **Praça do Giraldo**. Up until 1821 this broad arcaded square with its **Renaissance fountain** and 16th-century **Santa Antão** church was used for the execution of the victims of the Inquisition. **Café Arcadia** near the fountain is a good place to soak up the atmosphere of Évora. Narrow Rua 5 de Outubro leads north from here to the **Sé**. This cathedral, which demonstrates the transition from Romanesque to Gothic style, was built in 1186 and is certainly the most impressive of Portugal's medieval bishops' churches. The 14th-century Gothic **cloister** here is worth a visit as are the ★ **Museu de Arte Sacra** and the ★ **Museu Regional**. On the opposite side the raised ★ **Temple of Diana** with 14 granite columns is the only preserved Roman temple in Portugal. In the last century, after many years of misuse – once as an abattoir – the ancient structure was fully excavated and restored. Just alongside in a late-Gothic monastery stands the ★ **Pousada dos Lóios**. Some of the other main sights include the beautiful ★ **Largo Das Porta de Moura**, a picturesque square with a **Renaissance fountain** topped by a globe, ★ **Casa Cordovil** in a blend of Manueline and Moorish styles, and the ★ **São Francisco** church, with an unusual ossuary.

Temple of Diana

Return directly to Lisbon or continue along Route 5.

Route 5

Alto Alentejo and the Ribatejo

Estremoz – Vila Viçosa – Portalegre – Marvão – Castelo de Vide – Tagus Valley – Santarém – Lisbon (370km/230 miles) *See map pages 30–1*

Starting in and around Estremoz, this route proceeds in an arc to the north and back to Lisbon through the Alto Alentejo and Ribatejo regions.

Situated some 40km (25 miles) to the north east of Évora on the N18, the market town of ★ **Estremoz** is overlooked by an important Alentejan castle with a 13th-century keep. The huge market-place (Rossío), where traditional clay figures (*bonecos*) are sold, marks the entrance to the lower town. It is bordered by cafés and restaurants with **Aguias d'Ouro** highly recommended. High above in the upper town and with a fine ★ **view** stands the former castle. It now houses the **Rainha Santa Isabel** *pousada*. It was here that the wife of King Dinis, Rainha Santa Isabel, died in 1336 and a baroque memorial chapel is situated above.

Traditional pottery

About 12km (7 miles) to the southeast of Estremoz lies **Borba**. Now the centre of a wine-producing region, it seems to be a prosperous town – even the bus shelters are made from the locally-quarried marble. At the village of ★ **Vila Viçosa** 6km (4 miles) to the southeast, the **Palace of the Dukes of Bragança** welcomes visitors (conducted tours only). The striking Manueline **Porta do Nó**, or Knot Gate, is situated north of the palace.

The N4 continues eastward from Borba to the border town of ★ **Elvas**. It is an attractive town with some good hotels. The massive town walls remain in good condition as does the 843-arch aqueduct which still supplies water to the 17th-century **Misericordia fountain**.

Alter de Chão

From Estremoz, the E802/N245 initially heads through undulating countryside in a northwesterly direction to **Sousel**, but then follows a course due north to ★ **Alter de Chão**, a pretty town with a famous stud farm, and on to **Crato**. Turn right here into **Portalegre** at the foot of the Serra de São Mamede. This pleasant regional capital has a well-preserved old town and a carpet-making industry established many years ago by Pombal. For a taste of the regional cuisine, try **O Abrigo** at Rua de Elvas 74.

Portalegre carpet

A winding road heads northeast out of Portalegre into the ★ **Serra de São Mamede**, a nature reserve where it is said that bears still roam free. The land is still farmed in the traditional way with small fields and meadows among chestnut woods.

The N356 snakes its way up towards the Spanish border at Galegos but a few miles before the crossing point, the old fortress and town walls at ★★ **Marvão** will come into view. Situated 865m (2,837ft) above sea level, it provides a spectacular 360° panorama over the **Serra de Marvão** and across into Spain. The pretty town beneath the castle has retained its medieval character. There are a few small hotels here and the **Pousada Santa Maria** is situated by the entrance to the town.

Marvelling at Marvão

Descend from Marvão through chestnut and mock privet woods via **Escusa** to ★★ **Castelo de Vide**. This is another town that has managed to preserve its medieval character, dominated inevitably by a Moorish castle. The town authorities have kept building work on the edge of the town to a minimum and have also sought to restrict through traffic. The baroque **Praça D. Pedro V** in the town centre is overlooked to the right by the squat **Santa Maria** church. The main street ends with an attractive covered fountain, the 16th-century **Fonte da Vila**. A little further is the old Jewish quarter, where a 14th-century synagogue has survived. Climb up to the **Castelo** from where there is a fine ★ **view** over the rooftops and surrounding hills.

Castelo de Vide: the Jewish quarter

The N118 passes through **Apalhão** and **Tolosa** on its way west. In **Rossío** a road branches off to the north and becomes the N3. On this side of the Tagus and in a strategic position stands **Abrantes** with its interesting ★ **old town**. Stay on the N118, however, and follow the south bank of the river through the attractive roadside villages of the **Ribatejo** region. **Chamusca,** at the heart of a wine-producing region, is one such village; another is **Alpiarça** where the **Casa dos Patudos**, a grand villa dating from the turn of the century, houses an art collection belonging to its former owner. This fertile alluvial basin, the **Lezírias**, is famous for horse and cattle rearing. Not surprisingly, bullfighting still plays an important part in the lives of the local Portuguese 'cowboys'. The **Quinta da Alorna** in **Almeirim** is a horse-breeding and wine-producing farm which opens its doors to the public. At Martinmas in November a famous horse market and rodeo takes place in **Golegã** (on the other side of the Tagus).

Either cross over the Tagus at **Almeirim** and join the motorway at **Santarém**, the historic capital of the Ribatejo region – it is possible to link up with Route 1 at this point – or continue on the N118 towards Lisbon following on the south side of the river and passing through rural Ribatejo before joining the motorway near **Vila Franca de Xira**. This town is unquestionably the bullfighting capital of Portugal and during the first weeks of July and October hosts bull-running spectacles similar to the one held in Pamplona in Spain.

Botanical gardens at Coimbra

Route 6

Coimbra

Coimbra is full of history

The old university town of Coimbra (pop. 100,000) lies on the banks of the Rio Mondego. The university, one of the oldest in Europe and until 1910 the only one in Portugal, dates back to the 12th century. It switched between Lisbon and Coimbra several times, but in 1537 João III ordained that the university should occupy the former royal residence on the banks of the river. St Antonius of Padua, the poet Luís Camões and the dictator Salazar are all former students. With 20,000 students on roll, the university plays an important part in the local economy and the cultural life of the town. On special occasions students are obliged to wear black gowns or *capas*. The number of ribbons or *fitas* attached to the gown indicates years of study and the colour shows the faculty the student is attending, e.g. red is law, dark blue is the humanities. Every year in the middle of May, the *Queima das Fitas* takes place. This is a grand celebration with music that marks the end of examinations, the highlight being a fire for the ritual burning of the *fitas*. *Fado de Coimbra* is the Coimbra students' version of *fado* music, normally only associated with Lisbon. The songs are usually ballads, not so sentimental, but with more social and political comment and only sung by men. During the dictatorship, the protest song flourished in Coimbra, behind closed doors. *Grândola Vila Morena*, a song that became popular during the Carnation Revolution, originated in Coimbra from one of the *fadista*.

History

The name Coimbra is derived from the Roman word for the town, Conimbriga. But the site of the Roman town is at a different spot, some 16km (10 miles) away near Condeixa (*see page* 57). Germanic Suebi and Vandals destroyed this settlement during the 6th century but the inhabitants re-established their town on the Aeminium hill by the Mondego and retained the old name. During the 8th century Moors and Christians disputed the new settlement, but until the 11th century, with its population of Christians (Mozarabs), Moors and Jews, it served as an important trading post on the edge of Moorish territory on the Iberian peninsula. In 1064 the Christians finally won control and in 1139 Coimbra became the first seat of the new kingdom of Portugal. By the Middle Ages the town had developed into a respected centre of learning, although from the middle of the 16th century until the 18th century academic freedom was threatened by the influence of the Jesuits. From the 1960s onwards the university was a focus for dissent against Salazar and the revolution of 1974 was fomented by student demonstrations.

Sights

Unless otherwise stated, the monuments and museums are open from 9.30am–12.30pm, 2–5.30pm.

Largo da Portagem ❶, an old toll gate by the Santa Clara bridge, is a good starting point for a tour of the city. There is a large car park on the other side of the river. A busy shopping street, Rua Ferreira Borges, branches off to the north from here and this road effectively separates the historic upper town from the Baixa or lower town. Café Nicola at No 35 serves the best *arrufadas*, a local pastry.

The main gate in the medieval town wall still bears its Arabic name, **Arco de Almedina** ❷. A steep flight of steps known as the Quebra Costas or 'Backbreaker' leads up into the old town.

Café at Largo da Portagem

Rua Ferreria Borges

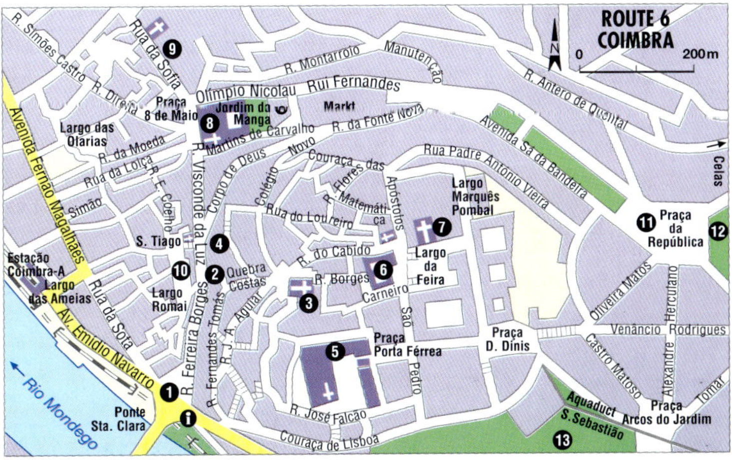

The upper town

Sé Velha

Azulejos outside the cathedral

Statue outside the University

The ★ **Sé Velha** ❸ or Old Cathedral with its crenellated walls of grey stone blocks resembles a fortress more than a house of God. It is nevertheless the most impressive of Portugal's Romanesque churches. Work started in the 12th century under the first king of Portugal, Alfonso Henriques. The huge structure is only broken up by the deeply recessed west doorway and window niches above, and by a weathered Renaissance **Porta Especiosa** doorway at the north side. The gloomy triple-naved interior (with some interesting ★ **capitals**) houses a superb Flemish ★ **altarpiece** with representations of the Assumption. In the ★ **Renaissance chapel** stand a number of tombstones. **Bishop Almeida's tomb** in the north apse was the work of Jean de Rouen. The **west gallery** has a fine wooden ceiling in Moorish tradition (1520). At the beginning of this century many baroque features were removed including several of the 15th-century *azulejos*. On the south side some steps lead up to the early Gothic **cloister**.

Cafés and restaurants surround the cathedral and a fine *azulejo* wall adorns the **Café Sé Velha**. Rua Coutinho leads north away from the cathedral to the **Palácio de Sobre Ribas** ❹, an old tower which was formerly part of the town wall and which possesses a fine Manueline portal and window surrounds. Another tower, **Torre do Anto**, is just a few yards away. It is now used as a craft centre.

Behind the cathedral more steps lead up to the ★★ **Old University** ❺. A double door from 1634, the **Porta Férrea**, marks the entrance to this ancient seat of learning. In the courtyard stands a statue of João III, the king who donated his royal palace to the university. Buildings line three sides of the courtyard, the fourth side offers a splendid ★ **view** over the river and the bank opposite. The Via Latina is a stepped colonnade leading to the **Sala dos Capelos** (Gown-wearers' Hall), the university's grand ceremonial hall. The baroque **clocktower** has a bell mockingly described as the *cabra* (goat). It was the victim of many student pranks when it rang to denote the start of the curfew and later the beginning of lectures.

Alongside the Manueline portal for the **university chapel** stands the colonnaded gateway to the ★★★ **Old Library**. Work started on it at the beginning of the 18th century on the instructions of João V who also commissioned Mafra (*see page 86*). This sumptuously decorated hall, the finest baroque room in Portugal, is painted in red, blue and gold. Delicate lacquer paintings cover the columns and balustrades. The royal artist himself looks down from the colourfully-painted ceiling at the richly carved mouldings and reading tables made from the finest Brazilian woods inlaid with mosaics. Some 120,000 volumes, including 2,000 manuscripts, fill the tall shelves.

Leave the university by the Porta Férrea. On the right-hand side are the modern university blocks built by Salazar in a barrack-like style, which tend to spoil the medieval atmosphere. On the left-hand side, Rua São Pedro leads down to the ★ **Museu Machado de Castro ❻** which is housed in the old Episcopal Palace. The basement contains some fine Roman cellars, while exhibits include a fine collection of sculptures and an 18th-century 'Bishops' Chapel'. The view from the Renaissance loggia is superb. The museum faces the Romanesque **São Salvador** (not open to the public) and the **Sé Nova ❼**, the new cathedral. The latter was built around 1600 as the church for a Jesuit college.

On the left-hand side of the Sé Nova a series of narrow alleys and lanes lead down to the ★ **Mosteiro de Santa Cruz ❽.** This former Augustinian monastery was founded in 1131 by the first Portuguese king, Alfonso Henriques, and his tomb is to be found in the choir. The complex originally covered a much wider area. In its early years it was an important cultural centre for the young kingdom and it was also the forerunner of the university. By the beginning of the 16th century the Romanesque monastery was in need of renovation and so Manuel I commissioned the finest interpreters of Manueline style, Boytac, Chanterène and the Castilho brothers. A magnificently sculptured ★ **portal facade** dates from this time, although the baroque **doorway** was added in the 18th century. The interior possesses some rich late-Gothic ★ **vaulting** and blue and white *azulejo* walls dating from the 18th century. In the choir the magnificently carved wall tombs, some 12m (40ft) high, contain the remains of the first Portuguese kings, Alfonso Henriques and his son Sancho. These tombs are the result of 10 years' work by the Manueline master, Nicolas de Chanterène (*see page* 85). The ★ **chancel** in pure Renaissance is also his work. The Manueline ★ **choir stalls** here are something of a rarity, as most church furnishings in Portugal were destroyed by Napoleonic soldiers. The ★ **sacristy** with 18th-century *azulejos* and a 16th-century ★ **painting** from the Portuguese school, and the **chapterhouse** with 17th-century *azulejos* open on to the ★ **Claustro do Silencio** or Silent Cloister, where the tracery on the arches is twisted into ropes, a common element of the Manueline style.

Outside the church in Rua Olímpio Fernandes stands an original ★ **fountain complex** (1533). Drawbridges lead from a central domed pavilion to four small round chapels which resemble watchtowers. Monks could withdraw here to pray and, once the drawbridges were raised, there was nothing to distract them. The whole structure symbolised the fountain of life (*fons vitae*) and the four rivers of paradise. On the other side of the road, the baroque

View over rooftops

Mosteiro de Santa Cruz

Azulejos everywhere

Fonte dos Judeus or Jews' Fountain marks the entrance to the old Jewish quarter. After the 16th century many Jews living in Coimbra were Marranos, meaning they had been forcibly baptised but still secretly adhered to the Jewish faith. They did, however, contribute greatly to academic life in the town. The last victim of the Inquisition in 1793 was one such Marrano, the dramatist António José da Silva, known in Coimbra as O Júdeu. Nearby in Rua Pedro da Rocha stands the former **Patio da Inquisição** or Palace of the Inquisition, now the headquarters of the Red Cross.

The lower town

On the other side of the Praça 8 de Maio – note the café in the Gothic vault of the former Santa Cruz refectory – is the **Rua de Sofia** ❾, a street with rows of 16th-century houses that are now protected by a preservation order. West of the main Rua Visconde/Rua Ferreira Borges axis lies the **Praça do Comércio** ❿ where in earlier days heretics were burnt at the stake. It is now the centre of the lower town and the city's commercial quarter. Attractive facades overlook the cafés which overflow on to the pavements. In the northeast corner of the square stands the Romanesque **São Tiago** church (1094).

Parque de Santa Cruz

Another road runs from Santa Cruz, past the market and the carefully tended gardens, by the Avenida Sá da Bandeira and up to the **Praça da Republica** ⓫ with its art nouveau facades and popular student cafés, such as **Pigalle**, **Académico** or **Moçambique**, favoured by Africans. The adjoining **Parque de Santa Cruz** ⓬ is an inviting place to take a rest. It used to belong to the monastery of the same name. The footpaths and steps, *azulejo*-covered benches and fountain were all places where monks could walk or sit in peace and meditate.

Jardim Botânico

Rua Alexandre Herculano heads south from here towards the **Jardim Botânico** ⓮ (daily 8am–6pm), the oldest botanical gardens in Portugal. The Marquês de Pombal founded the gardens in 1772. There are some fine old greenhouses on the upper terrace and a public area has been laid out like a palace garden with a late-baroque fountain and gateways. The subtropical plants in the garden include 40 varieties of Australian eucalyptus.

The other side of the Mondego

On the other side of the **Ponte de Santa Clara** bridge, Rua de Baixo leads off to the left towards the partly sunken Gothic ruins of the **Santa Clara-a-Velha** church. A number of attractive restaurants line the banks of the river here. In the 17th century, when it became clear that the old church could not be saved, the nuns set about building a

Exploring Conimbriga

new church, **Santa-Clara-a-Nova**. Not surprisingly they chose a spot well above the river and it can be reached via the Calçada de Santa Isabel. The ★ **view** from here extends over the town. Near Santa Clara-a-Velha lies **Portugal dos Pequenitos**, a children's park laid out in the Salazar years (Tuesday to Sunday 9am–5.30pm, closed Monday and public holidays). It contains miniature replicas of Portuguese and colonial buildings.

Rua Augusto Goncalves follows the river upstream to the **Quinta das Lagrimas**, the 'villa of tears'. In 1355 the unfortunate Inês de Castro and her children are said to have been murdered here by King Alfonso's bailiffs. Only the ★ **park** with its famous **Fonte dos Amores** (Love Fountain) is open to the public (daily 9am–5pm). The last line from one of Camões' poems which recounts the love story of Inês and Pedro I is quoted on a stone plaque. '...for tears are his drink, its name is love' (*see page 38*).

Quinta das Lagrimas

Conimbriga

The ★★ **ruins** of this Roman town – the biggest Roman excavation in Portugal – are situated 16km (10 miles) south of Coimbra and they can be reached by bus or car. The town lay on the Roman road that linked Felicitas Julia (Lisbon) with Bracara Augusta (Braga). Beautiful ★ **floor mosaics**, baths, swimming pools and underfloor heating demonstrate that the Roman settlers here enjoyed a high standard of living. One reconstructed garden contains raised flowerbeds and fountains. The defensive wall made from the fragments of destroyed buildings reflects the desperate struggle that took place between the Romans and the Germanic invaders. The Suebi tribe destroyed the town in the 5th century, in the next century the bishop's seat was moved to present-day Coimbra and all the inhabitants moved away. Near the site is an interesting **museum.**

Ruins of the Roman town

Route 7

Central Portugal

Aveiro – Buçaco – Dão – Viseu – Estrêla (390km/240 miles)

A quaint corner

Sea salt

This tour enters the Beira region from the Aveiro lagoon in the Beira Litoral and then goes inland to the Beira Interior – via the fairy-tale forest of Buçaco, the wine-producing Dão region and through Viseu into the Serra da Estrêla or the Star Mountains. This only requires a short detour before returning to the fast road from Viseu and then on to the main north-south motorway. The Beiras provide great variety within a small area. Distances are short, but the changes in landscape are quite dramatic.

Aveiro is an important port, a regional capital and a busy industrial centre. Its 70,000 inhabitants live by a large lagoon known as the **Ria de Aveiro**. The **old town** which faces the waterfront has grown up around the **Canal Central**. Salt is collected from the salt marshes and seaweed fishermen still sail into the lagoon in their special boats, the *barcos moliceiros*, which are characterised by flat hulls and high prows. The crew harvest the *moliços* from the brackish water and sell it as a fertiliser. Aveiro's earlier prosperity came from salt, cod fishing and maritime trade, but in 1575 a storm created sandbanks offshore that left the town cut off from the sea. The townsfolk suffered badly as a result and it wasn't until 1808 that a new channel reconnected the lagoon to the sea. The main sight of historic

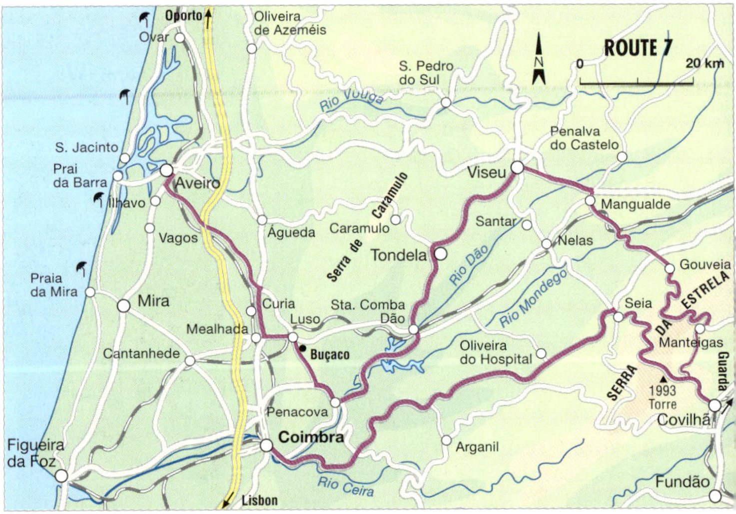

interest is the **Convento de Jesus** (now **Museu de Aveiro**) which has a particularly rich display of *talha dourada*.

The lagoon's spits extend for 30km (19 miles) as far as **Ovar** in the north – look out for house fronts with *azulejo* decorations – and for 25km (16 miles) to the south Surfing is popular at **Furadouro** and **Torreira** beaches and **Costa Nova** boasts some colourful fishermen's huts. The local speciality is *enguia* (eel). There are a number of ways to explore the lagoon: on foot, by bicycle, car or bus. In summer, ferries link the spits between São Jacinto and Barra.

To continue the journey into the Serra da Estrêla either head due east to **Albergaria** and Viseu via the N16 highway or else take a more circuitous route along the quieter roads initially via **Ílhavo** (and the porcelain-manufacturing centre of **Vista Alegre** nearby) and ★ **Curia** by the N1 (spa town with shaded park and some fine *belle epoque* hotels). At the junction of the N1 and the turning to Curia stands one of the best-known restaurants in Portugal, **Pedro dos Leitões**. Sucking pig or *leitão assado* is the speciality here and it should be eaten with a locally-produced **Bairrada** red wine. One Bairrada vineyard in the **Quinta do Carvalinho** near **Mealhada** has apartments to rent. At Mealhada take the N234 inland past the spa town of **Luso**. Certain mineral waters are highly prized commodities in Portugal and Luso water is one of Portugal's best-selling labels. Many Portuguese prefer to fill plastic containers with the untreated water that flows from the taps by the roadside near Luso than use mains tap water.

Palace Hotel do Buçaco with mural detail

Luso lies beneath the ★★ **Buçaco Forest**. It is now a 480-ha (1,185-acre) National Park, although it has been carefully guarded and maintained for centuries. In a central clearing stands a former ★ **hunting lodge**, now the **Palace Hotel do Buçaco**. The building was commissioned by the king and plans were drawn up by a stage architect in grandiose neo-Manueline style. Work started in 1884 but the monarchy was ousted before it was finished, so a court chef bought the property and turned it into one of the plushest hotels in the country.

The forest has been a refuge for monks since the 6th century. Carmelites built a monastery here in the 17th century and the **Tapada do Buçaco** was surrounded by a huge wall. Papal edict forbad any woman from entering the park on pain of excommunication and also decreed that no tree was to be felled. Exotic plants thrived in the damp micro-climate and the monks amused themselves by growing sub-tropical species that had been brought back from the colonies. The huge Goan cedars, for example, date from the 17th century. In 1810 the park was the scene of

Village in the Serra de Caramulo

Dão vineyard worker

a decisive battle between Napoleon's army and an Anglo-Portuguese force led by Wellington. In 1834 all religious orders were abolished and the monks expelled from the forest. Happily, the government took over responsibility for the management of the forest and it now contains 400 native and 300 exotic plants and trees.

Penacova, a little town south of the Buçaco Forest above the **Rio Mondego**, makes a good base for walks. The **Lorvão** monastery stands in a delightful spot. Coimbra (*see page 52*) is 22km (14 miles) downstream and it is possible to make the journey by hired kayak. Ask for details at the *turismo* by the Miradouro do Terreiro.

Follow the N2-E801 northward out of Penacova to **Santa Comba Dão**, which is the centre for the vineyards producing the famous Dão wine and also the site of Salazar's grave – still a place of pilgrimage for some Portuguese. The road now passes through woodland and vineyards before reaching **Viseu** (41km/26 miles). At about halfway take a detour into the ★ **Serra de Caramulo**. This lonely range of hills is overgrown with heathers and mimosa and the summits of the **Caramulinho** and **Cabeça da Neve** (both around 1,000m/3,250ft) offer tremendous ★ **views** of the surrounding countryside. The main town in the hills is **Caramulo**, a faded spa still favoured by those convalescing from lung disorders. The **Museu de Automóvel** (Tuesday to Sunday 10am–12.30pm, 2–6pm) draws many visitors to the town. Many of the vehicles on display here date from the earliest years of the motor-car. One of the exhibits is the Mercedes that Hitler presented to Salazar. To get to the Caramulinho, take the **Avenida Abel de Lacerda** which becomes the N230-3. About 3 km (2 miles) further on a signpost indicates the footpath to the summit (30 minutes).

The next stop is ★ **Viseu** (pop. 22,000), the administrative capital of the Dão region. This important town has a long history. It was the centre for the Lusitanian resistance fighter **Viriatus** in his struggle against the Romans. It was here too that **Roderich**, the last Visigoth king, was defeated by Islamic invaders. His grave is to be found in **São Miguel do Feital**. As is so often the case, the new outer suburbs are as forbidding as the defensive wall would have been to potential attackers.

Fortifications at Viseu

The historical old town in Viseu is still intact and can be reached from the busy **Praça da República** (Rossío). The **Adro da Sé** with its grey granite **cathedral** lies in the heart of the old quarter. The stern effect of its box-like Romanesque structure is scarcely diminished by the simple, early baroque facade. Inside, unique Manueline knotted rope ★ **vaultings** are supported by Romanesque pillars. The Renaissance arcades in the ★ **cloister** have a distinctly Classical look.

A must for art lovers

The white baroque facade, rounded gable and squat spires of the **Igreja da Misericordia** create a striking contrast with the drab cathedral. The former episcopal palace near the Sé now houses the **Museu Grão Vasco** and it is a must for art lovers (Tuesday to Sunday 10am–12.30pm, 2–5pm). Around 1500 Viseu was a centre for Portuguese painters and one of its most celebrated exponents Vasco Fernandes or Grão Vasco lived and worked in the town. The gallery displays works by the Viseu School and paintings by modern and contemporary Portuguese painters. A number of other interesting little corners await discovery around the cathedral square. A Viseu art connoisseur and collector by the name of Almeida Moreira lived just off the Praça da República and the **Casa Museu Almeida Moreira** now exhibits some of his prized possessions. **Rua Direita** is the main shopping street and the place to buy a few bottles of Dão, the celebrated local wine. Visitors in search of some unusual souvenirs should seek out the big market that takes place between mid-August and mid-September on the occasion of the **Feira de São Mateus**.

East of Viseu on the N16 lies **Mangualde**, a town which boasts a number of old country houses with beautiful gardens. One of the finest is situated on the edge of the town and is open for visitors. The ★ **Palácio dos Condes de Anadia** (October to August, Tuesday to Sunday 9am–noon, 2–6pm) dates from the 18th century and behind its pink facade, it possesses a fine collection of *azulejos*.

Serra da Estrêla

Head southeast out of Mangualde, cross the Mondego River and carry on as far as **Gouveia**, the starting point for a tour of Portugal's highest peaks in the ★★ **Serra da Estrêla**, a granite mountain range 60km (35 miles) long and 30km (20 miles) wide, formed by Ice Age glaciers.

The villages on the stony slopes are ringed by small chestnut woods and fields and stand out like oases in a gloomy landscape of poor pastureland and bare plateaux. At higher altitudes, jagged walls of rock tower up above boulder-strewn slopes and bizarrely-shaped cirques. This region, once thinly populated by shepherds and their flocks, is now Portugal's only skiing centre. Ample facilities for tourism have encouraged summer visitors too, with camping, fishing and walking all popular pursuits.

The N232 climbs out of Gouveia, where *cão da serra*, the local sheepdogs, are bred, into wild mountain terrain and up to the **Pousada de São Lourenço** at an altitude of 1,290m (4,230ft). Cheap accommodation – with some marvellous views – is available at the **Penhas Douradas** weather station (1,383m/4,540ft), which is situated 4km (2½ miles) before the *pousada*. The road then descends rapidly into the **Rio Zêzere Valley** and **Manteigas** (755m/2,475ft), another good base from which to explore the *serra*. Good souvenirs include the local ewes' cheese (*queijo da serra*), wool and sheepskins. The **Poço do Inferno** (Hell's Well) nearby is a waterfall which cascades down into a cavern.

Guarda Cathedral with detail of interior

The N338 from Manteigas follows the dead straight Rio Zêzere Valley upstream as far as the junction with the pass – the highest road in Portugal – that runs through the middle of the *serra*. Follow the road signs to Covilhã. After about 4km (2½ miles) **Penhas de Saúde** at 1,500m (4,900ft) comes into view. Unfortunately, unplanned tourist development has seriously blighted the landscape. The small industrial town of **Covilhã** (pop. 18,000), the southern gateway to the *serra*, is not particularly inviting either but the *turismo* on the Praça de Município and the **Clube Nacional de Montanhismo** issue leaflets on itineraries for mountain walks.

The N18 runs from Covilhã to **Guarda** further north. Once the site of a border fortress, Guarda at 1,065m (3,490ft) above sea level is the highest town on the Iberian peninsula. The town is rather unflatteringly described as *forte, feia, fria e farta* – strong, ugly, cold and smug.

For the return journey, ignore the signs to Manteigas but carry on as far as the **Torre** (1,993m/6,537ft), the highest peak in the *serra*. Although often shrouded in mist the plateau at the summit has parking facilities. **Lagoa Comprida** reservoir on the northeastern side of the Torre is the longest expanse of water in the *serra* and the mountain village of **Sabugeiro** a little further on is well known throughout Portugal for its sheep-milk cheese. In the **Casa da Sofia** it is possible to watch the cheese being made. **Solar dos Oliveiros**, an 18th-century country house near **Seia**, is another place where visitors can watch the local cheesemakers at work.

Oporto seen from the river

Route 8

Oporto

Like Lisbon, **Oporto** stands at the mouth of a river just before it opens out into the Atlantic Ocean, but the Douro Valley is deep and narrow, so the banks are higher and steeper and the old town smaller, with a confusing maze of streets at its heart. Four bridges link Oporto with Vila Nova da Gaia, the headquarters of the port wine industry on the south bank. Two of the bridges are reinforced concrete structures, but the other two are iron, and date from the 19th century. Ponte de Dona Maria Pia was by Gustave Eiffel in 1876, the other, Ponte Dom Luis I, was constructed a few years later in a similar style. That this bridge has become popular with bungee jumpers is an indication of the depth of its span. The best picture postcard views of Oporto old town, clinging to the tall granite rock, may be enjoyed from here or from the terrace of the Nossa Senhora do Pilar church on the south bank. At river level the pretty Cais da Ribeira displays its colourful facades and washing blowing in the breeze. Just above lie the densely-packed dwellings of the Bairro da Sé, itself overlooked by the formidable lead-grey cathedral and the huge barrack-like Episcopal Palace with the tower of the Clérigos church emerging from a maze of roofs in the background. At street level the contrast between poverty and prosperous refinement, oriental-style chaos and European sobriety, is particularly striking.

Oporto's iron bridges date from the 19th century

History

Oporto is Portugal's second city and has about half a million inhabitants (1.5m in Greater Oporto). Not only has it given its name to one of Portugal's best-known exports, port, it also gave its name to the whole country.

The Moors christened the land between the Douro and the Minho Portucale, after a Roman settlement known as Portus (Latin = port) on the left bank of the Douro and Cale (Greek *kalos* = beautiful) on the right bank. When the Moors were driven out in the 11th century, the kingdom of Portugal emerged from the Christian province of Portucalia. Oporto had always been an important trading centre but after the reconquest, around 1050, it became the main commercial centre in the north. By the 13th and 14th centuries, trading routes with England, Flanders and the Hanseatic League had become well established. Close ties with England – the king hoped for English assistance against Castilian aggression – led to the first alliance, with the signing of the Treaty of Windsor in 1386, and in the following year the marriage of King João I to Philippa of Lancaster in Oporto cathedral. Their famous son, Henry the Navigator, the driving force behind the Voyages of Discovery, was born in Oporto in 1394.

The riverside wharves

Sandeman's famous sign

English merchants trading in goods from the Portuguese colonies, such as tobacco and sugar, were welcomed in Oporto. The relationship between the town and England flourished and there are still many examples of English influence in the city, with the Methuen Treaty of 1703 strengthening links. This notorious agreement opened up the British market to Portuguese wine in exchange for British textiles, thus destroying the Portuguese textile industry. The big names in the port trade are mainly English, e.g. Sandeman, Cockburns, Forrester, Taylor and Offley.

In Oporto, unlike Lisbon, the middle-class merchants played, and continue to play, an important role in the community. The principal reasons for this are the restrictions which were imposed on the nobility in the early Middle Ages and which extended into the 17th century. They were not allowed to stay in the town for more than three days and were prohibited from building any *palácios*. The king himself was not even allowed to have a residence, only the right to reside at the episcopal palace. The town also won rights for its citizens from the bishop. But Oporto tried in vain to resist the centralising demands from Lisbon. Protests against the establishment by the Marquês of Pombal of a Portuguese company with monopoly control were put down with violence, and a military governor, João de Almada, was promptly installed. But his appointment proved to be a blessing in disguise. Many measures to redevelop, improve and extend the town in the second half of the 18th century can be attributed either to him or to his son Francisco.

A spirit of progressive liberalism was growing among the citizens. In the 19th century, Oporto was the breeding ground for an anti-royalist movement. A new constitution was declared as early as 1822. Nearly 70 years later, in 1891, the first, albeit unsuccessful, republican uprising took place here. The emergence of the Salazar dictatorship was certainly not welcomed in Oporto.

The city's self-confidence has resulted in a local economy which, despite a smaller population, remains as strong as that of Lisbon. Oporto is the centre of the steel and petrochemical industries and has many important textile and fish processing factories. Leixões, the industrial port, is the second biggest in Portugal and the workforce here has a reputation for hard work and moderation – the latter quality is responsible for the nickname for Oportans, *Tripeiros* (tripe eaters). Every Portuguese is familiar with the expression: Lisbon is for living it up, Oporto is for working, Coimbra is for studying and Braga is for praying. It is true that the citizens of Oporto take a much more sober view of life and the city has undoubtedly suffered from always coming second after Lisbon. The people feel they are spoon-fed from the capital where all the political and administrative decisions are made. A sense of resentment against the capital has thus been responsible for the revolutionary demands, unrest and rebellions.

Oporto is best explored on foot

Sights

Motorists are advised to leave cars in their hotel car parks or in the south bank town of Vila Nova da Gaia, as Oporto is famous for its overcrowded and labyrinthine streets. Anyway, with its flights of steps, narrow alleys and steep slopes, Oporto is best visited on foot. Contrasting images range from the Neapolitan atmosphere of the crumbling Ribeira quarter to the grandiose Palácio da Bolsa

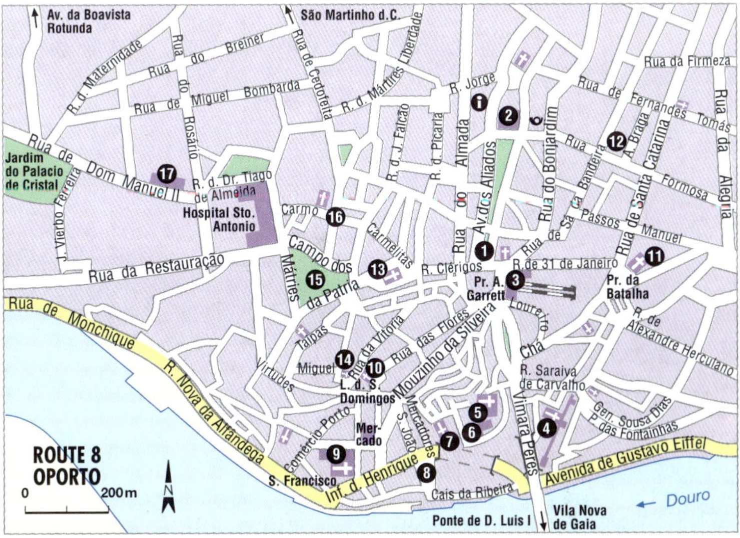

Praça da Liberdade

(Stock Exchange), from shopping streets that are still ordered according to trades, the colourful Bolhão market, art nouveau and *azulejo* façades with wrought-iron balconies, to dubious dives, sardine sellers and shoeshines, backyards with crowing hens, old-fashioned shops and cafés with a faded charm.

A flourishing nightlife on Lisbon's scale is less easy to find. The young people here generally head for the discotheques in the fashionable Brasilia shopping centre or for Foz do Douro.

Start out from **Praça da Liberdade** ❶ at the lower end of the broad **Avenida dos Aliados**. This square stands at the heart of the city's commercial quarter and is surrounded by some imposing turn-of-the-century buildings. At the upper end is the **Câmara** ❷ or Town Hall. Built in 1920, it is crowned with a 70-m (230-ft) high bell tower. At the centre of the square stands an equestrian **statue of Dom Pedro IV**. On the night of 24 June the popular Festival of St John, one of many curious local customs, takes place here. On the east side of the Praça, the **Café Impérial** with its 1930s decor is well worth a visit. Try a *cimbalino*, an espresso coffee Oporto-style, either from here or from another art deco café **A Brasileira** in Rua do Bonjardim, in preparation for the steps and steep slopes that lie ahead.

The Cathedral and the Ribeira

An underpass runs from **Praça da Liberdade** across to the old **São Bento** station ❸ where the entrance hall is decorated with some large *azulejo* designs. The Congregados church stands diagonally opposite and its front was tiled with *azulejos* at the same time. Take a detour to the right of the station in an arc along Rua do Loureiro, lined with shops and bars, Rua Chá, and then off to the left into Rua Saraiva de Carvalho. Hidden away in Largo de 1 de Dezembro lies **Santa Clara** ❹. This small chapel is covered with shimmering gilded carvings, one of the finest examples of ⋆ **talha dourada**.

The city wall

Ponte de Dom Luis I

Behind the archway to the left of the church are the remains of the city wall, dating from the 14th century. The ⋆ **view** from here extends along the Douro, deep below, and across its bridges. The ⋆ **Ponte Maria Pia** railway bridge by Gustave Eiffel spans the valley to the left. This served as a model for the **Ponte de Dom Luis I** directly below, whose iron arch (172m/564ft wide and 68m/223ft deep) carries two road tracks. A path, Passeio dos Fontainhas, runs beneath Santa Clara along the banks.

Return via Avenida de Alfonso Henriques to Oporto's cathedral or **Sé** ❺ (daily 9am–12.30pm, 3–6pm), crowning the highest point of the granite rock on which much of the old town is constructed. It was built as a defensive fortification in the 12th century and resembles the cathedrals of Lisbon and Coimbra. Despite some extensive alterations it has retained its fortress-like appearance. Alterations which were carried out in the 17th and 18th centuries have resulted in a rather gloomy interior. The highlight here is fine baroque Altar of the Sacrament made from 800kg (1,760lbs) of embossed silver. The small 14th-century Gothic cloister has some delightful ★ **azulejo** frescoes from the rococo period.

Azulejo frescoes in the cathedral cloister

Nicolau Nasoni, an architect of Italian origin, was responsible for most of Oporto's 18th-century baroque buildings, including the **Episcopal Palace** with its 60-m (200-ft) facade, situated just behind the cathedral, and also the elegant ★ **Casa Museu Guerra Junqueiro** ❻ in Rua de D. Hugo (Tuesday to Saturday 11am–12.30pm, 2–5.30pm), a narrow alley that winds around the east side of the cathedral. This museum, once the residence of the revolutionary hero and satirist Guerra Junqueiro (1850–1923), preserves the lavish lifestyle of the writer, who was also a keen collector of *objets d'art*. A flea market is held every day around the **Calçada Vandoma** just beneath the cathedral.

Bairro da Sé

The descent into the lower town begins past the medieval tower in front of the cathedral. The walk passes the **Bairro da Sé**, one of the poorest parts of the city – the attractive facades conceal dingy living quarters in decaying houses. A long flight of steps down bare rock leads to the Largo do Colégio where the impressive front of the 17th-century Jesuit **Igreja dos Grilos** ❼ towers up like a rock face.

Follow Rua da Santana and Rua dos Mercadores down to **Praça da Ribeira** ❽ by the old river port. This old quarter has become a popular haunt for visitors to Oporto. Many of the houses have been restored and there are numerous cafés, restaurants and shops. Cruises up the Douro, including the 'Four Bridge Cruise' or two-day trips into the port-producing regions, sail from here. Near the bridge a plaque decorated with flowers and candles serves as a reminder of a tragedy that occurred here during the Napoleonic invasion. The bridge carrying hordes of fleeing townsfolk collapsed. Thousands of them were thrown into the river and drowned. The narrow alleyways behind the Ribeira quayside have become the territory of drug-dealers and prostitutes and they are best avoided. The decline set in during the 1960s when the port facilities were moved downstream. The São Nicolau parish is now in receipt of funds donated by the European Union for a wide-ranging project which is aimed not only at renovating 2,000 homes but also at meeting some of the social needs within the community.

Praça da Ribeira

Port wine cellars of Vila Nova da Gaia

Vila Nova da Gaia

Only a short stroll from the Ribeira quayside across the lower roadway of the **Ponte de D. Luis** lies Vila Nova da Gaia, headquarters of the port trade for over 300 years. Many of the lodges welcome visitors who will be invited to sample the port. The most famous, **Porto Sandeman** at Largo Miguel Bombarda 3, houses a unique museum documenting the history of the company. Shallow skiffs, the *barcos rabelos*, sway gently by the quayside, advertising the various companies. These boats were used to carry the barrels down the Douro. A regatta during the Festival of St John on 24 June is the only occasion when they can be seen working.

Vintage port

Oporto's commercial quarter

Wealth and poverty are separated by **Rua do Infante Henrique**, where Henry the Navigator was born (Caso do Infante). This road used to be called Rua dos Ingleses (Englishmen's Street). Alongside the shipping agents and on the corner with Rua de São João, stands the 18th-century **Feitoria Inglese**, a grand English merchants' club only open to members. But it was not just the British who wished to keep their business private. The Oporto traders formed themselves into elite clubs such as the Ateneu, Clube Portuense or the Golfclub. Opposite the **Feitoria Inglese** stands the city's business centre, the ★ **Palácio da Bolsa** (Stock Exchange) ❾ with its grandiose neo-Moorish reception hall known as the ★ **Sala Arabe** (conducted tours Monday to Saturday 9am–noon, 2–5pm). It was constructed on the site of a Franciscan monastery and the ★ **São Francisco** church to the rear is probably the finest in Oporto. Built around 1400, it is richly ornamented with 17th- and 18th-century *talha dourada* gilded carvings.

On the way back, take a stroll through the pretty **Rua dos Flores**, the gold and silversmiths' street. **Pedro A. Baptista** at No 235 specialises in both antique and modern jewellery and is perhaps the most famous shop in the street. The **Misericórdia Church** ⑩ on the left-hand side displays one of Portugal's finest ★ **Renaissance paintings**. It shows Manuel II, with his wife and eight children. Ask at the adjoining house for the key.

By tram to the sea

The terminus for the No 1 tram (Infante) is situated outside the Franciscan church. The old *eléctrico* trundles its way through the picturesque **Miragaia** district along the banks of the Douro to the smart **Foz Velha** suburb and the 300-year-old **Castelo de Queixo**. The industrial district and resort of Matosinhos is just a little further on. The route back on the 18 tram from Castelo de Queixo in the direction of Boavista is probably more interesting. Break the journey at the junction of Avenida da Boavista and Avenida M. Gomes da Costa. At the Casa da Serralves in Rua de Serralves 977 stands the new **Museu de Arte Moderna**. This splendid 1930s villa and garden houses works by some celebrated French masters of art deco (Greber, Ruhlmann and Lalique). Return to the town centre along Avenida de Boavista where most of the newer hotels are situated, and the Rotunda da Boavista, one of the city's busiest junctions. The **Centro Comercial Brasilia**, Oporto's newest temple to consumerism, is situated here.

Rua Santa Caterina

Shopping streets

North of Praça da Liberdade a series of *avenidas* lead northwards. **Rua do Almada** was named after the military governor who was responsible for planning the city streets in the 18th century. It is the street of ironmongers, while **Rua da Picaria** is the road of cabinet makers. **Rua de Sá da Bandeira** contains a variety of different shops, but **Rua Santa Catarina** which runs parallel and is partly pedestrianised is the main shopping street. The **Majestic** at No 112 (closed Sunday) dates from 1922 and is the most famous of Oporto's traditional cafés. The 100-year-old **Grande Hotel do Porto** was once the finest in town. **Rua da Santa Catarina** ends at **Praça da Batalha** by the **San Ildefenso church** ⑪. It was built in the 18th century but the *azulejos* are from the 1920s. Of the three old cinema halls here, only the facade of the **Aguia d'Ouro** (1899) remains, while the grander **São José** (1908) and the **Batalha** (1940s) are still in use. The entrance to the ★ **Mercãdo do Bolhão** ⑫, the biggest food market in Oporto, is in **Rua Formosa**, a busy link road between Rua

Grande Hotel do Porto

Santa Catarina and Avenida dos Aliados. To appreciate the atmosphere in full, make a tour of the gallery inside and then explore all the open-air stalls.

The western inner town

Torre de Clérigos

The view from the tower

Torre de Clérigos ⓭, a 75-m (250-ft) church tower, the tallest in Portugal (daily 10am–noon, 2–5pm), has become a symbol for the city. Its great height was intended to help guide the port ships back into harbour. Nicolau Nasoni built the oval church (1732–48) and the tower (1755). He now lies buried within. It is possible to climb to the top of the tower and enjoy a superb ★ **view** in all directions.

Take a stroll through Rua do São Bento da Vitória, past the huge 17th-century former convent as far as the small **Nossa Senhora da Vitória** ⓮ which also offers a fine ★ **view** over the rooftops with their glass light domes (*claraboias*). Stop for a moment at the house on the corner of **Rua de São Miguel** and admire the 17th-century *azulejos* which show scenes from everyday life. Take Rua das Taipas into the bumpy Rua das Virtudes to Passeio das Virtudes from where there is yet another ★ **panorama** over the river. A small park, **Jardim João Chagas** ⓯, which is flanked by the vast **Palace of Justice** built during the Salazar regime, and the 18th-century **Hospital Santo António**, leads into **Praça Gomes Teixeira** ⓰ with palm trees, fountains and two Carmelite churches (17th- and 18th-century). The external *azulejos* date from 1912. Rua do Cedofeito heads north from here and at the end about 1km (½ mile) away stands the modest **São Martinho do Cedofeito** church. Dating from the 6th century, it is the oldest church in Portugal.

Oporto's biggest art museum, the **Museu Nacional Soares dos Reis** ⓱ (Tuesday to Sunday 10am–1pm, 2–5pm), is to be found behind the Hospital Santo António in Rua D. Manuel II. Exhibits include the work of Portuguese artists from the 16th to 19th centuries, as well as pottery, glass and silverware. Further west on Rua D. Manuel II lie the flower-filled gardens of the **Palácio de Cristal** and the **Palácio dos Desportos**, a large arena for sporting events. Rua de Entre Quintas runs along the west side of the park. Take a close look at No 220, the **Quinta da Macieirinha** and its attractive garden. This enchanting 19th-century mansion houses the **Museu Romantico** (Tuesday to Saturday 10am–1pm, 2–5pm), fully furnished in the style of a 19th-century Portuguese house. The ground floor accommodates the **Solar do Vinho do Porto**, the Oporto Port Wine Institute (Monday to Friday 11am–11pm, Saturday 5–11.30pm), the ideal place to round off the tour as over 150 different varieties of port are available for sampling.

Route 9

The Minho

Guimarães – Braga – Barcelos – Viana do Castelo – Valença do Minho – Peneda-Gerês – Ponte de Lima – Braga (410km/255 miles) *See map pages 72–3*

The ancient province of Minho, the historic heart of Portugal, lies in the northwest of the country and is famed for its greenery – for its green coast, its green landscapes and its green wine (*vinho verde*). The people enjoy the biggest festivals and markets in the country, good food, the best vineyards and a traditional rural lifestyle. In the far northeast lies the Peneda-Gerês National Park with some very old village communities and lonely footpaths.

Guimarães (pop. 70,000), some 50km (30 miles) from Oporto (*see pages 63–70*), is now a thriving industrial town with a proud history but it sometimes likes to describe itself as the 'cradle of Portugal', being the birthplace of **Alfonso Henriques** who proclaimed the county of Portucale, the land between the Minho and the Douro, as the kingdom of Portugal. Above the town on the 'Holy Hill' stands the turreted **castle** (Tuesday to Sunday 9am–12.30pm, 2–5pm), the 27-m (88-ft) keep where Alfonso was born in about 1110, and the simple **São Miguel** chapel where he was later baptised.

Paço dos Duques

Descend from the castle past the **Paço dos Duques**, the Palace of the Braganças – altered extensively during the Salazar years – to the Rua de Santa Maria in the ★ **old town** with its houses of weathered granite, wooden verandas and broken paving slabs, where the town's history lives on. Two museums are certainly worth mentioning: **Museu**

Toy exhibition, Guimarães

Martins Sarmento in Rua Paio Galvão (Tuesday to Sunday 10am–noon, 2–5pm) houses some interesting finds from the Celtic-Iberian settlement of Citânia de Briteiros (*see below*); and the **Museu Alberto Sampaio** (Tuesday to Sunday 10am–12.30pm, 2–5.30pm), which is accommodated in an old cloister, part of a Dominican monastery, by the delightful **Largo de Oliveira** square in the old town. Many of the fine paintings and sculptures on display here are by Portuguese artists from the 14th–16th centuries. One of the two *pousadas* in Guimarães is situated in an adjoining building. The other *pousada* in the old **Santa Marinha** monastery, 7km (4 miles) outside the town by the **Monte Penha** panorama, offers particularly luxurious accommodation.

Largo de Oliveira pousada

In Guimarães, St Walter's Festival (*Festas Gualterianas*) is held on the first Sunday in August.

Near **Caldas das Taipas** about 8km (5 miles) past Guimarães on the road to Braga, a turning branches off to **Citânia de Briteiros**, the excavated site of a Celtic-Iberian settlement (daily 9am–6pm).

Braga (pop. 130,000) is a proud city – conservative and loyal to the church. As well as being the seat of the Primate of Portugal, it is also an important industrial centre. Bracara Augusta was a busy crossroads and administrative centre even in Roman times. However, the charmless new town and the almost permanently congested streets have to be negotiated before it is possible to admire the quiet calm of the ★ **old town** with its 30 or more churches and palaces and the maze of narrow alleys and pretty squares. Originally a Romanesque construction, the **Cathedral** is now a mixture of styles encompassing several centuries. The 14th-century **Capela dos Reis** contains the tomb of Henry of Burgundy and his wife Teresa, the parents of Portugal's founder Alfonso Henriques. On the other side of the pedestrianised Rua do Souto stands the **Palácio dos Biscainhos**, a traditional 18th-century mansion with a beautiful garden (Tuesday to Sunday 10am–noon, 1–5.30pm).

Stopping for a drink presents a difficult choice between the various old-style cafés in the vicinity of the otherwise dull Avenida da República, the **Astoria**, the **Vianna**

Square in Braga

Steps to Bom Jesús do Monte

Cockerel souvenirs at Barcelos

Stone cross with cockerel

or the **O Nosso Café** where the action continues until late at night. About 4km (2½ miles) outside the town along Rua Boavista lies an art historian's dream, the 7th-century Visigoth chapel of **São Frutuoso**. It is one of the few churches in Portugal to show a Byzantine influence.

Another famous church in the vicinity is the ★ **Bom Jesús do Monte**. After Fatima, Bom Jesús (5km/3 miles from Braga) is the most important place of pilgrimage in Portugal. An imposing ★★ **flight of steps** built during the 18th century leads up to the church entrance (564m/1,850ft). There are a number of ways to make the ascent: an old funicular railway – itself a museum piece; by car or on foot up a winding road; or by the steps – and a true pilgrim will climb the latter on his or her knees. **Monte Sameiro** (584m/1,915ft), another pilgrims' church, also stands at the top of long flight of steps and at the end of a lengthy woodland path. Facilities here include a restaurant and the spot also offers a fine ★ **panoramic view**.

If travelling at Easter, do not miss Braga's impressive *Semana Santa*.

Barcelos, some 20km (12 miles) west of Braga on the N103, lies on the banks of the **Rio Cávado**. This small town is a centre for the manufacture and sale of pottery, *santons* or carved wooden yokes and also the *galo*, the Barcelos cock. Plenty of examples of these will be on sale at the huge **market** – said to be the biggest in Portugal – that takes place here every Thursday. The story behind the cock, a medieval legend, concerns a pilgrim who had been accused of theft and was sentenced to hang. When the pilgrim appealed to St James for help, the cock on the hangman's dinner plate was made to crow as proof of the pilgrim's innocence. The judge set him free and in gratitude the pilgrim constructed a monument which can be seen in Barcelo's **Paço dos Duques de Bragança** museum.

The municipal park by the pretty river bank is the perfect place for a rest. The **Centro Artesanato** at the tourist information office in the Torre de Menagem, Largo de Porta Nova, displays a wide range of handicrafts.

Costa Verde is the name given to the stretch of coast between Oporto and the Spanish border. The shoreline is practically one long, unbroken beach bordered by sand dunes and pine trees. Sadly, this coast has in recent years been a target for developers and walls of concrete now overlook the beach. **Póvoa da Varzim** and **Vila do Conde**, with an attractive old town and a good beach, have now almost merged thanks to the construction of new hotel blocks. **Ofir**, by the lagoon at the mouth of the Cávado, is a new tourist village boasting a marvellous beach.

Viana do Castelo, Monte Santa Luzia

Eposende, on the opposite bank, has also been transformed. However, in **São Bartolomeu do Mar** and further north, it is still possible to find a quiet beach. Sun worshippers need to be reminded that they do not always get what they are seeking on the Costa Verde. It can be quite cool and windy. Fog often envelops the coastal towns even in summer. Try a ride on the coastal railway line, particularly between Viana do Castelo and Caminha.

Praça da República

Viana do Castelo (pop. 20,000), 25km (16 miles) further north, is the biggest population centre on the coast. The Romans called this port at the mouth of the Rio Lima 'Pulchra' or 'Beautiful'. It may be hard to justify this description after a short drive through the new town, but there is no doubt that the ★★ **old town** is one of the finest in Portugal. Many of the old buildings here date from Viana's heyday in the 16th and 17th centuries, particularly those around the attractive **Praça da República** with its ★ **Renaissance fountain** (1551), the **Town Hall** and the ★ **Casa da Misericórdia** (1589), an unusual late Renaissance hospice with open loggias supported by grotesque caryatids. The part of town between the Praça and the promenade is worth a closer look as there are many Manueline features to identify. In the third week of August, the baroque **Nossa Senhora de Agonía** chapel in **Rua do Rego** is the setting for one of Portugal's most popular *romarias*, for which the women wear colourful, embroidered costumes.

A ferry crosses to the splendid **Praia do Cabelo** beach. Information about boat trips on the Rio Lima can be obtained at the *turismo* in Rua do Hospital Velho.

One of Viana's distinctive landmarks is the **Monte de Santa Luzia** some 5km (3 miles) north of the town. A neo-Byzantine pilgrims' church with a fine view can be reached by car or by an old funicular railway. Guests at the luxury Santa Luzia hotel can enjoy some marvellous views.

View from Santa Luzia

Vila Praia de Ancora, 15km (9 miles) north of Viana, is a pleasant fishing village and seaside resort with a sandy beach extending from here to **Moledo**, some 20km (12 miles) away. The northernmost coastal town is **Caminha**, site of the old border fortress at the mouth of the Minho.

Colourful Caminha

The recently improved N13 passes through **Vila Nova da Cerveira** (*pousada* in the fortress) and vineyards before reaching **Valença do Minho** some 27km (17 miles) further on. This town is the main border crossing into northwest Spain. The ★ **old town**, still completely ringed by walls, is a fine example of old Portuguese architectural style. On Wednesday, market day, the town is overwhelmed by Spanish shoppers in search of bargains. Early evening is a better time to appreciate the town.

The route now branches off inland along the Minho into the isolated northeast corner passing more vineyards and pine forests. The centre of *vinho verde* country is **Monção** and, like most towns on the Minho, it is dominated by a fortress which surveys the border. Its long history consists mainly of skirmishes with the neighbouring Spaniards. Even the grand spectacle that takes place in the town on Ascension Day, in which the inhabitants enact St George's fight against the dragon, probably reflects the conflicts that the townsfolk have had to endure.

Follow the N101 for some 3km (2 miles) through the countryside and past the distinctive vine pergolas as far as **Arcos de Valdevez**. Here stands the imposing **Palácio da Brejoeira**, a wine lodge set in extensive gardens. Unfortunately, it is not open to the public, so the beautiful garden has to be viewed from outside the walls.

Melgaço, 25km (16 miles) east of Monção, is situated high above the Minho. It is said that the best *vinhos verdes* come from this remote corner of the region. In August the carnival spirit takes over with folk groups from all over Portugal descending on the town.

Serra do Gerês waterfall and an inquisitive local

In Melgaço the EN202 snakes its way uphill, first, after 8km (5 miles), to the **Quinta do Hospital** and then on to **Lamas de Mouro** and **Castro Laboreir**, where a fine ★ **view** over Galicia opens out. Lamas de Mouro is the northern entry point for the **Peneda-Gerês National Park**. This mountainous border region with peaks of up to 1,500m (4,920ft) covers an area of 72,000ha (178,000 acres). It has been a protected nature reserve since 1971. The western part is used for the cultivation of maize and rye and also as grazing pasture, with approximately 15,000 people living in the villages and hamlets scattered over the hillsides. Old thatched stables remain in use as do the unusual *espigueiros*, little granite grainstores on stilts for drying cereals and maize. Vegetation thrives up to about

1,200m (3,900ft) but beyond that the skyline is dominated by wild rocky peaks. Megaliths, Roman milestones and Romanesque church ruins are testimony to a rich cultural past stretching back thousands of years. The eastern side of the park, the wettest region in the whole of Portugal, has become a haven for some unusual species including golden eagles, wolves and foxes. Some rare plants have gained a foothold here too. Around **Pincães** and **São Lourenço** the remains of primeval oak forest can still be found.

Information for visitors can be obtained from the tourist information offices in Oporto, Braga, Caldas do Gerês and the park access points in Lamas de Mouro, Terras de Bouro (Arcos de Valdevez) and Mezio (Gerês). Warning: road maps are not very accurate. A suggested itinerary through the park is as follows: Lamas de Mouro – Peneda (detour to the overgrown baroque pilgrims' church of **Senhora da Peneda**); Peneda – Soajo (30km/19 miles of fairly difficult road); Soajo (café and restaurant) – Lindoso (the starting point for walks by the **Vilarinho dos Furnos** reservoir and the **Portela do Homem** pass); Lindoso – Entre-Ambos-os-Rios (park exit) – Ponte de Barca.

Ponte de Barca is a pretty town by the River Lima. Make a quick detour to the Romanesque chapel at **Bravães** 4km (2½ miles) away to admire the remarkable ★ **doorway**.

Ponte de Lima, 18km (11 miles) further on, is another attractive town with a Gothic bridge built on Roman foundations. On the second Monday of every month a market is held on the banks of the river under the plane trees. The first market was held here in 1125 and it is thought to be the oldest in Portugal. Enjoy a drink outside one of the cafés around the **Praça de Camões** near the old bridge. The old town lies behind the riverside watchtower and it is worth taking a stroll through the narrow alleys, up steps and past some fine 16th-century town houses.

Ponte de Lima is the headquarters of Turihab, the agency for accommodation in older, historic premises. There is a wide and interesting range to choose from.

The southern entrance to the National Park is at the spa town of **Caldas do Gerês** which can be reached from Ponte de Barca by taking the N101 to the south and then following the north bank of the Rio Cávado. The reservoirs in this region with their fjord-like inlets supply the energy needs of the Oporto-Braga region. There is a *pousada* above the **Caniçada** reservoir. **Gerês** makes a good base from which to explore the National Park along waymarked footpaths.

Return to Braga on the N103 or else take the opposite direction beside the reservoirs to **Chaves** and join up with Route 10.

Terrain for goats

Maize mounds at Lindoso

Ponte de Lima

Amarante Bridge

Bathing in the river

Route 10

The Douro and Trás-os-Montes

Amarante – Lamego – Pinhão – Miranda do Douro – Bragança – Chaves – Vila Real – Amarante (550km/340 miles) *See map pages 72–3*

Allow plenty of time for this route. It follows narrow winding country lanes through an attractive rural landscape. The tour starts in the wine-producing region of the Douro Valley, where vineyards with grapes for making port line the steep, terraced hillsides overlooked by the baroque mansions of the wealthy landowners. For centuries, the river was the only link between Trás-os-Montes and the coast. Even today, it can be a long and tortuous journey into the barren, primeval land 'beyond the mountains', where summer is scorching hot and winter long and hard. It comes as no surprise to learn that many of its inhabitants have left.

An old arched bridge (1790) spans the **Rio Tâmega** linking both parts of the small town of ★ **Amarante**, and branches from plane trees and willows overhang the water by the river banks. Rowing boats can be hired here. The patron saint of Amarante, São Gonçalo, is also the patron saint for those in search of a partner and married women hoping to conceive. On the first weekend in June, pilgrims pay homage at his grave in the 16th-century **monastery church of São Gonçalo**, a building with a granite facade that dominates the old town. The *gonçalos*, the phallic-shaped biscuits which are sold during the festival, probably have their origins in a pre-Christian fertility cult. The *turismo* is housed in the monastery alongside the **Museu Municipal** where some remarkable works by the Portuguese Cubist Amadeu de Sousa Cardoso (1887–1918) are displayed. Cardoso spent some time in Paris sharing a studio with Modigliani.

For the journey on to Bragança, do not take the IP4 highway via Vila Real, which is currently being improved, but leave Amarante on the N15 and turn off along the N101 to the southeast. This road crosses the ★ **Serra de Marão** as far as the pretty town of **Mesão Frio**, noted for its red wine. The Douro town of **Pêso da Régua** is 10km (6 miles) further on.

Régua is the commercial centre of the port wine region and the headquarters of a number of port companies. The **Casa do Douro** which oversees the types of vines used in the production of port also welcomes visitors, who will be invited to sample a glass of port in the traditional *cálice*. A journey along the Douro Valley by train is an unforgettable experience.

Make a 12-km (7-mile) detour south of the Douro to ★ **Lamego**, an attractive episcopal town with a large, stone-grey cathedral. Although it has 12th-century Romanesque foundations, these have been subject to a number of alterations. Among the exhibits in the **Museu Regional** which is housed in the episcopal palace opposite are five paintings by Grão Vasco (*see page 61*). Little remains of a **Moorish castle** on a hilltop above the town apart from a 13th-century keep and a section of the walls. The main attraction in Lamego, however, is the holy sanctuary of ★★ **Nossa Senhora dos Remédios**. This place of pilgrimage stands on a 600-m (1,975-ft) high terrace at the top of a grand flight of 685 steps (*escadaria*), similar to that at Bom Jesús near Braga (*see page 73*). The steps, terraces, chapels, statues and the sumptuous ★ **facade** of the baroque church at the summit combine to create a colourful and harmonious whole.

Steps of Nossa Senhora dos Remédios and statuary

Lamego is also famed for its **Raposeira** sparkling wine (cellars open Monday to Friday).

Stay on the south bank of the Douro when returning. **Pinhão**, 25km (16 miles) to the east, is the centre of the port wine region and some of the best vineyards are located in the surrounding area. Ancient customs, music and dancing play a part in the celebrations to mark the end of grape picking in October. The station at Pinhão is adorned with a splendid collection of *azulejos*.

Sabroso, the birthplace of Magellan, lies a few miles north of Pinhão on the N322. Some 4km (2½ miles) further on, just outside Vila Real, is **Mateus** where Mateus Rosé, one of Portugal's most famous exports, is produced. The magnificent baroque palace that appears on the label (and the garden) is open to visitors (daily for conducted tours 9am–1pm, 2–6pm).

Return to Pinhão and then follow the road initially northeast in an arc through **Alijó** and then down to **Tua** where the road briefly meets the Douro again. A journey on the narrow gauge railway through the Tua Valley to **Mirandela** is thoroughly recommended. Journey time is about 1½ hours.

The N214 now leaves the Douro Valley and meanders for 37km (23 miles) as far as ★ **Vila Flor** which possesses some interesting monuments including a Roman fountain.

Continue via bustling Torre de Moncorvo all the way to the quiet town of ★ **Miranda do Douro** (pop. 2,000), which occupies a rocky hill above the deep valley of the Douro. The old town has recently been smartened up, its populace surviving on the light flow of border traffic. For many centuries there was no contact of any kind between the communities on either side of the border. A fortress (in ruins) once occupied the strategic position overlooking the river valley but now a dam blocks the flowing water and the power which is generated from the turbines meets about a quarter of Portugal's requirements. In this remote region around Miranda, a strange dialect known as *Mirandês* is still in use.

On the road to Bragança

View from the castle

Follow the N218 over a barren and lonely plateau for another 84km (51 miles) as far as **Bragança** (pop. 18,000) in the far northeastern corner of Portugal. Bragança castle and its huge **Torre de Menagem** (belfry) survey the town from a prominent position. The castle was built in 1187 by **King Sancho I** and was regarded as more or less impregnable. Dwellings, gardens and a church have since found a home inside the walls. The ★ **Domus Municipalis** is a unique structure. It was built as a sort of town hall in Romanesque style in the 12th century but on an irregular pentagonal ground plan. The **pelourinho** (pillory column) at the main entrance is supported by a granite wild boar. Sturdy sculptures such as this one date from Celtic-Iberian times and they are fairly numerous in the north of the country. The municipal museum also displays three of these unusual *porcas*. The most famous of all stands on the main square in Murça.

The ★ **castle** was the seat of the Bragança family that ruled Portugal from 1640 to 1910. The best view of the castle is from the *pousada*. The small, historic ★ **old town** with its 16th-century cathedral and central *avenida* with pavement cafés has been well preserved. The **regional museum** in Rua Serpa is well worth a visit (closed Monday). In the settlements of the **Montesinho Nature Reserve** and on the other side of the border in Spain, an unusual Iberian-Romance dialect survives.

The N103 which links Bragança with Chaves (103km/63 miles) is one of the most spectacular roads in Portugal. It snakes through broad upland plain providing some breathtaking views. Some 4km (2½ miles) outside Bragança, it is well worth making a short detour to **Castro de Avelã** where the brick ruins of a Romanesque monastery now serve as a home for the village church. The road climbs steeply through **Vinhais**, a town with some traditional wooden balconies, as far as **Rebordelo**.

After a succession of hills and valleys **Chaves** (pop. 15,000) eventually comes into view. The name derives from the Portuguese word for 'key'. A glance at the map will reveal how the town occupies a key position on Portugal's northern border. In Roman times it was known as Aquae Flaviae after the hot springs which are still used in the treatment of rheumatism. Two Roman milestones on the bridge testify to its great age. Heavy through-traffic and the unsightly new town should not deter the visitor from taking a walk around the old town. At its centre is **Largo de Camões** which is ringed by impressive facades. Busy little streets lead off in all directions from the square. Chaves is famous for its cooked meats, in particular *presunto,* a very tempting variety of smoked ham.

Chaves

There are a number of sights within reach of Chaves, including **Outeiro Seco** (5km/3 miles), where the chapel contains some interesting ★ **frescoes**, and **Boticas** where the *vinho dos mortos* is stored in the ground. The Quinta da Mata 3km (2 miles) outside the town near **Nantes** makes a good base for further exploration of the area..

Passing green reservoirs and dark pine forests, the magnificent landscape on the N103 from Chaves to Braga has something of a north European feel.

Return to Amarante on the N2 through Vila Real. **Vidago**, only a few miles out of Chaves, is renowned for its thermal baths, used to treat internal conditions, and an art nouveau palace hotel. **Pedras Salgadas**, a little further on, has a 1910 casino.

Biscuit eating contest at Vila Real

Vila Real is an important administrative centre by the **Rio Corgo**. Set in attractive countryside, the old town is always lively. This 'Royal Town' was the seat of several noble families and their **coats-of-arms** adorn the fine town houses. A new university here specialises in agriculture, so the next generation of farmers should be better equipped to transform the backward agricultural methods currently employed in Trás-os-Montes.

Coat-of-arms

The **Serra de Alvão** nature reserve and the tranquil **Basto** wine region are both within easy reach of Vila Real.

A fast road leads west out of Vila Real to Amarante and on to the coast at Oporto.

126

Art History

Art in Portugal can be admired as much from the road as in a museum. More important than individual churches, palaces or museums is the unspoilt unity of the whole – often the entire central area of a town or village. In many cases, the village houses cluster together beneath the shadows of a castle alongside a winding road that follows the contours of the landscape.

Houses in the south are white-washed often with blue or yellow wall edging 'to keep the evil spirits away' and are covered by red-tiled roofs lightly curved at the ends. In the north the grey of slate and granite dominates. The *quintas*, the magnificent country mansions ringed by extravagant gardens, are found mainly around Lisbon and the wine-producing regions. *Azulejos*, the brightly-coloured glazed tiles, can be seen in wall decorations all over Portugal. Introduced by the Moors, this popular art form has been used ever since as an adornment for churches, country houses and stations.

Opposite: a fine facade in Alfama, Lisbon

Azulejos are encountered all over Portugal

Roman and Arab influences

Evidence of the four centuries of Roman occupation and even more years under Arab rule is hard to find. A few aqueducts, the Temple of Diana in Évora and the ruined town of Conimbriga are clearly Roman. Moorish culture has left nothing to compare with the grand buildings that still survive in Spain. The Portuguese language, which derives principally from Latin but also has a good sprinkling of Arabic words, is the chief legacy of the early occupying forces.

Early monarchy: knights and the Romanesque style

Shortly after the Moors took the Iberian peninsula by storm in the 8th century, the struggle (*reconquista*) to restore Christianity began in the north, but it was another 300 years before the small Christian enclave of Portucalia was established between the Minho and the Douro. The Portuguese monarchy was founded in 1140 by the young count Alfonso Henriques and his army of Christian knights when they succeeded in pushing the Moors back to the Tagus. In 1178 Alfonso Henriques ordered work to commence on the massive early-Gothic monastery of Alcobaça. It was built in honour of the Cistercians whose help was decisive in the Battle of Santarém (1147) and who played a significant part in winning papal recognition for their country. Today it serves as a monument to the founding of Portugal.

King Alfonso Henriques was of Burgundian extraction and had close links with the Cluny monastery in Burgundy that had sponsored the crusader knights who led the fight

Alfonso Henriques and his knights

against the 'infidel' in Spain and Portugal. It is hardly surprising then that the churches which were built following the *reconquista* are Romanesque in style. Portugal's early churches were simple structures resembling castles and often made from unadorned granite. The old cathedral in Coimbra is a good example of a fortified church.

With Portugal forced to defend itself on two fronts against Moors and Castilians, castles sprang up all over the country, many of which still lie in ruins on the hilltops. King Dinis (1279–1325) saw off the Moorish threat, and independence from Castille was secured, at least for the time being. The all-important step in the struggle for independence from Spain during this period was the Battle of Aljubarrota in 1385. The huge monastery of Batalha, a masterpiece of Flamboyant Gothic, was built as a memorial to this event.

King Dinis

Under Dinis, the first Portuguese king who could read and write, the economy gained ground and a Portuguese culture emerged. He struck the first trade deal with England and laid the foundations for the special relationship between the two countries that continues to this day. The far-sighted king planted a large pine forest in Leiria and in later generations the wood was used to build the caravels for the Voyages of Discovery

Voyages of Discovery to world power

Cloister at Belém

Belém, the great monastery at the mouth of the Tagus which was started in 1500, was built to commemorate the discovery of the sea route to India in 1499 by Vasco da Gama, and the rise of Portugal as a maritime power.

Portugal's finest hour was the period of the Voyages of Discovery. The pioneer for these journeys was Henry the Navigator, third son of João I, the victor in the Battle of Aljubarrota. He founded a nautical school in Sagres and gathered together information and experts from all over Europe in order to explore hitherto unknown lands, using Portuguese ships.

At the time of these momentous discoveries, Portugal was ruled by Manuel I (1495–1521). 'O Venturoso' (the Lucky One), could now call himself not just the king of Portugal but also 'Lord of Guinea, Lord of Maritime Travel, the Conquests and Lord of Ethiopia, Arabia, Persia and India'. As a symbol of his domination of the world, he chose the armillary sphere, a globe with rings representing the equator and the path of the sun and stars. Manuel I's reign was a period of success in all areas. Even the harvests were said to be the best in living memory. In the 16th century Lisbon was the finest metropolis in Europe. Every year 2,000 ships sailed up the Tagus laden with jewels, spices, silks and black slaves. One-fifth of the merchants' profit was taken by the king.

The arts flourished and at Manuel's court, where the king enjoyed erudite conversations to the accompaniment of beautiful music, worked Gil Vicente, Portugal's first great poet and creator of modern comedy. Architecture known as the Manueline style was the first bold and original expression of Portugal's self-confidence. It manifested itself in Gothic tracery of intertwined and knotted rope, in anchors, corals, seaweed and shells, in lotus blossom and other Oriental and Indian motifs. It reflected the mystery of the sea and the exotic world of distant lands. Other favourite features were the armillary sphere and the eight-sided cross of the Knights of the Order of Christ that adorned the sails of the Portuguese caravels. The finest examples of Manueline style are the monastery and tower at Belém, the Capelas Imparfeitas and the cloister at Batalha and the chapterhouse and window in the monastery of the Knights of the Order of Christ in Tomar. Diogo Boytac, João de Castilho and Francisco de Arruda were the architects mainly responsible for the creation of these masterpieces. The Frenchmen Nicholas de Chanterène and Jean de Rouen copied French developments from late-Gothic to Renaissance.

Batalha interior

Claustro do Cimeterio at Tomar

Decline and Spanish dominance

Portugal's luck could not last. It sounds unbelievable but the vast wealth that the country had accumulated led eventually to impoverishment. With a total population of only a million the departure of so many people to the new colonies was simply too big a drain on manpower. The fields were left untended and the arrival of so many goods from abroad choked off any incentive to manufacture products at home. The new-found wealth was frittered away by royalty and noblemen and nothing was invested in the country's infrastructure. Under Manuel's successor João III, foreign banks were used to finance investment in colonial ventures and then interest had to be paid out of the profit from the imported goods. The eviction of the Jews and the Inquisition in 1536 ruined the economically active middle classes. With the arrival of the Jesuits came the *auto-da-fés* and repression. Drought, famine and plague followed. Many people emigrated to Brazil.

An unhappy crusade to Morocco against the Moors by the young King Sebastião led to humiliating defeat at the hands of a vastly superior force at Alcazarquivir in 1578. Any vestiges of Portuguese military power disappeared with this ill-fated venture. Only 60 soldiers out of an army of 18,000 returned from the battlefield and the childless Sebastião, the last member of the royal family, was reported missing. In 1580 Phillip II of Spain, taking advantage of the power vacuum, invaded and seized control. In the same year Luis de Camões, author of the famous epic poem the *Lusiads*, died of the plague in Lisbon. Portugal remained under the Spanish yoke for 60 years from 1580 to 1640 and the country not only had to endure the ignominy of Spanish occupation, it also suffered the loss of important colonies and trade routes, to the English and the Dutch. During this difficult period the missing Sebastião was proclaimed as 'O Desejado' ('the longed for') – somehow it was felt that his return would restore Portugal's battered fortunes. Sebastião, of all people, the leader who had blindly led the country to disgrace, was presented as a national saviour.

Under Spanish rule the Jesuit style of ecclesiastical architecture gained a firm foothold. Felipe Terzi, an Italian architect, is credited with the monumental church of São Vicente in Lisbon. Manueline exuberance gave way soon after Manuel's death, to a cold and austere Renaissance style with Italian overtones. Ornamentation was replaced by plain geometrical shapes. Only the *azulejo* tile allowed artists the opportunity to embellish and elaborate.

Cathedral at Oporto

Azulejos cover a whole facade

Splendour and extravagance

With English support national sovereignty was won back in 1640 under the third Bragança dynasty. At the end of the 17th century new treasures from abroad started to flow back into a devastated country. Gold and diamonds from Brazil provided untold riches. João V, Portugal's 'Sun King', was seduced by the fantastic wealth and he set about squandering it on a series of major projects. The huge monastery palace at Mafra, meant to surpass the Spanish El Escorial in splendour, became a symbol of his regal delusions of grandeur. Artists and architects were commissioned from Germany, Italy and France. The leading architects at Mafra were the German, Johann Friedrich Ludwig, and his son Peter. In Oporto the Italian Nicolau Nasoni was placed in charge of the building work. The Braganças were responsible for the introduction of the baroque style to Portugal. Churches and mansions with curving gables and pointed towers started to appear, adorned with blue-white *azulejos* and *talha dourada*, the gilded wood used to decorate altars and chapel walls. The best examples of *talha dourada* can be seen in São Francisco in Oporto, the Jesús monastery in Aveiro and Santo António in Lagos. Portuguese baroque exerted a major influence on Brazilian architecture.

In the meantime the queasy Portuguese economy continued to decline. In 1703 the notorious Methuen Treaty with England was signed, a trade agreement which was unquestionably a disastrous deal from the Portuguese point of view and which led to further stagnation.

On the morning of All Saints' Day in 1755 a terrible earthquake destroyed Lisbon, inflicting serious damage even as far away as the Algarve. The tidal waves and fires that later reduced the centre of the capital to rubble claimed the lives of 20,000 people and wrecked 300 *palácios*, 110 churches and the royal palace. The man of the hour was a minister by the name of José de Carvalho, later ennobled to become the Marquês de Pombal, a leader of unlimited energy. The rapid reconstruction of the city was due entirely to him and the new lower town became known as the Baixa Pombalina. At the same time Pombal initiated a set of major reforms on taxation, measures to boost the economy and plans to expel the Jesuits, but they had been only partially implemented by the time he was deposed in 1777.

End of the monarchy, dictatorship and revolution

The 19th century brought catastrophe. Napoleonic troops occupied and plundered the country. What had been spared by the earthquake, was now destroyed by French soldiers. The royal family fled to Brazil and did not return until 1821. In the interim Portugal was virtually an English colony. Political instability and conditions close to civil war lasted until the monarchy abdicated in 1910. There were 44 changes of government between 1910 and 1926, but before long Portugal found itself under the control of the former Minister of Finance, a supporter of the fascist regimes in Germany and Italy. António Salazar ruled Portugal for almost 40 years and, while he provided much-needed stability, his domestic policies ensured that Portugal remained economically backward. Wars in Angola and Mozambique also took their toll on lives, the economy and the people's patience, culminating in the so-called Carnation Revolution in 1974 which cast aside the authoritarian regime of Salazar's successor. Since then Portugal has enjoyed democratic rule and now looks to the EU for financial support and economic guidance.

The early 19th century was a tumultuous time

The architecture of the 19th and 20th centuries reveals the different faces that have ruled from Lisbon. In the Salazar years, art deco and grandiose fascist architectural styles prevailed. Portuguese painting and sculpture had little influence on European movements, but *azulejo* designs became an important form of expression for popular artists, and railway station concourses and other public places became *azulejo* galleries. Eça de Queiroz, a writer who was influenced by Flaubert, dominated Portuguese literature in the 19th century. Fernando Pessoa, an important poet who conveyed something of the melancholic Portuguese mood in the first half of the 20th century, was not discovered outside Portugal until after the Carnation Revolution. Other contemporary writers include José Saramago, Lobo Antunes, Miguel Torga, José Cardoso Pires and Agustina Bessa Luis.

Food and Drink

Portuguese cuisine consists of plain, straightforward fare based around fish, meat and cabbage. Unlike Mediterranean dishes, fresh herbs do not play an important part. Traditional Portuguese dishes include *caldo verde*, a thick potato and cabbage soup, and *bacalhau*, dried cod served in a multitude of ways.

Although dried cod, now mainly imported from Norway, is a national dish, fresh fish is very popular too. *Sardinhas* (sardines), *carapaus* (small mackerel) and *lulas* (squid) are often barbecued or baked. *Robalo* (sea bass) is often served in fish restaurants by the coast and *pargo*, *sargo* and *tamboril* (varieties of bream) are also plentiful. Freshwater fish such as *truta* (trout) and *lampreia* (river lamprey) appear on menus, especially in the north. *Caldeirada* is a nourishing fish soup and *arroz de marisco*, a dish with rice and a variety of fish and shellfish, resembles paella.

Bife (beef) and *porco* (pork) are cooked and served in a variety of different ways. *Borrego* (lamb) and *cabrito* (kid) has a more delicate flavour and is often braised. *Frango* (chicken) makes a very enjoyable meal as most Portuguese poultry comes from free-range farms.

Potatoes or rice are usually served with the meat or fish. Carrots, cauliflower and perhaps a few French beans are boiled, then coated in butter. Otherwise, vegetables are added to soups, rather than served as accompaniments.

For dessert, there is usually only a small selection of cheeses available in restaurants with *queijo do serra* perhaps the best known, but this is often replaced by the blander *tipo serra*. However, the Portuguese love sweet desserts (*doces*). Monastery bakeries have spawned many varieties of cakes often bearing unusual names such as 'heaven's bacon' and 'nuns' pastries'. Sugar and egg yolk are the principal ingredients with coconut, marzipan, almond and cinnamon adding extra flavour. *Bolo de amêndoa*, an almond cake with soured cream, is worth trying. A *cafezinho* or a small brandy such as *bagaceira* or *aguardente* usually finish off a good meal.

Meal times

Hora do almoço is to Portugal what the *siesta* is to Spain. Most restaurants will be packed full from noon until 3pm and diners will often choose the bargain 'dish of the day' or *pratos do dia*. Supper is usually served from 8pm.

Wines

The range and quality of Portuguese wines is one good reason for a visit. Whether red or white, a simple *vinho da casa* or a special *reserva*, a lightly sparkling *vinho verde*

Opposite: fish drying in Nazaré

Grilled sardines

Try some vinho verde

or a full-bodied port – all taste good and come at very affordable prices. The best-known DOC regions are **Bairrada**, **Colares**, **Dão**, **Douro**, **Setúbal** and **Vinho Verde**. The wines from the Alentejo are beginning to attract attention. *Fonseca* from **Azeitão** is one of the best-known names in the world of Portuguese wine.

Port

Port

Vinho do Porto has become something of a symbol of Portugal. Port is a fortified red or white wine, usually but not always served with cheese or a dessert and with a 20 percent alcohol content. It is produced from grapes grown on the terraced slopes of the Douro Valley between Régua and the Spanish border. Many of the famous brand names are English, such as Cockburn, Forrester and Offley. English domination in port production dates from the Methuen Treaty of 1703 which handed over all production and trade in port to English merchants.

Restaurant selection

Pousadas offer fine dining

The following suggestions from the most popular centres are listed according to three categories: $$$ = expensive; $$ = moderate; $ = cheap.

Albufeira
$$Jardim d'Allah, Beco J.B. de Sousa. In the town centre with romantic inner courtyard. **$$Cabaz da Praia**, Praça M. Bombarda 7. Clifftop view.

Alcobaça
$$Trindade, Praça D. Alfonso Henriques. Fish restaurant.

Amarante
$$$Zé da Calçada, Rua 31 de Janeiro. Top-class restaurant with terrace by river.

Aveiro
For fresh fish, try **$$Centenário** and **$$Galo d'Ouro** at Aveiro market.

Cascais fish restaurant

Cascais
$$$Estalagem do Farol. Nostalgic villa in an isolated position on the edge of town by the sea.

Coimbra
$$Dom Pedro, Avenida Emidio Navarro 58. Coimbra's top restaurant, near the *turismo*. Serves *chanfana*, kid braised in red wine, a Coimbran speciality. **$Zé Manel**, Beco do Forno 10/2. *Sopa da pedra* (stone soup) is the speciality in this student bar. Hot stones are placed in the soup to keep it warm.

Évora
$$Guião, Rua da República 81. A good reputation for Alentejan cuisine.

Faro
$$Café Chelsea, Rua de Fr. Gomes 28. Plenty of atmosphere. Two storeys.

Guimarães
Many good restaurants in the town. Try **$$Nicolino** by the Largo Toural.

Lunchtime in Guimarães

Lisbon
Paying a lot of money for food does not always mean eating well. There are many small, reasonably-priced restaurants that serve excellent food. **$$$Tavares Rico**, Rua da Misericórdia 35. Grand room with gilded mirrors. **$$$Alcântara Mar**, Rua M. Luísa Holstein 15. Popular venue in a warehouse by the harbour. Table reservation essential. **$$Cervejaria Trindade**, Rua Nova da Trindade 20. A traditional beer hall in a former monastery. **$$Pap'Açorda**, Rua Atalaia 57. Fashionable spot. Imaginative cuisine. Table reservation essential. **$Bonjardim**, Travessa de Santo Antão. Large, family restaurant.

Eating al fresco in Lisbon

Oporto
$$$Portucale, Rua da Alegria 598. Beautifully decorated roof-top restaurant serving Portuguese cuisine. **$$Aquário Marisqueiro**, Rua Rodrigues Sampaio 179. One of Oporto's top fish restaurants. **$$Tripeiro**, Rua Passos Manuel 195. Serves Oporto tripe specialities, such as Tripas á modo do Porto.

Setúbal
$$Bocage in the square of the same name. Serves typical Portuguese fare.

Sintra
The restaurants in the district of São Pedro de Sintra are good and not as tourist-orientated as those in the centre.

Tomar
$$A Bela Vista, near the old stone bridge. Try the restaurant's speciality: grilled kid.

Viana do Castelo
Many restaurants to suit all tastes.

Viseu
$$A Veranda da Sé, Rua Augusto Hilario 55. Modern bistro in old premises.

It doesn't have to be fado

Follow the signs

Folk dancing

Nightlife

Fado is a nostalgic music, a popular art with a long and mysterious history. Authentic *fado* has its roots in Lisbon. Once associated with working-class neighbourhoods, it is now of mixed appeal, with tourists often a primary commercial target. The *fadista*, a powerful-voiced singer, is usually backed by *guitarras* – the twelve-stringed Portuguese version, and *violas* – what we would call guitars. The Portuguese say it takes more than a good voice to become a *fadista* – it takes soul as well. Fado houses usually serve dinner (optional) and often charge a fairly steep entrance or minimum consumption charge. Singing starts around 10pm. It's best to reserve in advance.

Lisbon

Portugal's nightlife is liveliest in Lisbon, and Lisbon's nightlife – from *fado* to disco – throbs in the Bairro Alto. Start off in a *fado* restaurant such as **Adega Machado** or **Adega Mesquita**. The best discos in Lisbon are to be found by the river on Avenida 24 Julho between the Ribeira (around the market) to Alcântara by the Tagus Bridge. With 100,000 Africans living in Lisbon, African music has a large potential audience. **Banana's Power** and **Kudissanga** are recommended but **Gartejo** and **Alcântara** are without doubt the top venues.

The weekly newspaper *Sete* contains advice on restaurants, cultural events, etc.

Oporto

The Ribeira is handy and fun: the **Postigo do Carvão** is a restaurant and piano bar. **Aniki-Bobo** – no food, but good music – is next door. In the Boavista area, the Centro Comercial Dallas has a couple of *boîtes*, **Splash** and **Flying Dutchman**. In the Centro Comércial Brasilia is **Griffon's** with a disco on one level and a quieter bar on another. The smart set goes to **Swing** (Praceta Engenheiro Amaro Costa), another two-level disco/pub.

Coimbra

This is a city of young people so there are discos, but the local brand of *fado* is also very popular. Among the best places: the **Trovador**, a restaurant in the Largo da Sé Velha, the **Boémia** bar at Rua do Cabido, 6, the **Diligência**, a bar off Rua do Sofia, and the late-night **Agora**.

Towns and smaller cities – anything smaller than Oporto – tend to go to sleep at about 10pm or 11pm, and you'll find very little to do besides a long, slow dinner or going to a disco. There are two exceptions: the tourist towns, and the resorts in the Algarve.

Traditional woven goods

Shopping

The most famous Portuguese handicrafts are ceramic tiles (*azulejos*) and pottery, Arraiolos rugs, and embroidery and lace work. Different varieties of ceramic work are produced all over the country. While many regional crafts are sold in Lisbon, there is usually a wider and more authentic selection in the provinces.

Alentejo
Cane and wicker work, cork products (baskets, coasters and sculpture), wool blankets, Arraiolos rugs, ceramics (*barro*), traditional hand-painted furniture, copper goods and lace.

Algarve
Palm and wicker work, copper and brass articles, candles, earthenware pottery.

Coimbra and the Beiras
Ceramics (colourful animal motifs from near Coimbra; elegant Vista Alegre porcelain from the Aveiro region; black clay pottery from the Viseu region); woven rag quilts (from the Serra da Estrêla); as well as lace and embroidery.

Douro and Minho
Ceramics, wickerwork, straw baskets and hats; embroidery, crochet, and regional costumes (especially from the Viana do Castelo area), religious art (from Braga). The Thursday market in Barcelos, north of Oporto, has lots of handicrafts for sale.

Trás-os-Montes
Blankets; weaving and tapestries; crocheted bedspreads; black pottery from Bisalhões (near Vila Real).

Ceramics from Alçobaca

Getting There

Opposite: the classic image

By air

TAP Air Portugal is Portugal's national airline and it has wide international links. Moreover many major airlines make non-stop direct flights to Lisbon from capital cities in Europe and elsewhere. You may also, from some countries, fly directly to Oporto in the north and Faro in the south. Links with London are particularly good. There are several flights a week from New York, and from Boston. Between regular airlines and charter companies the choice is considerable – and ticket prices variable.

All three airports also have regular bus services to their city centres. Portela Airport is located 13km (7 miles) north of Lisbon. Buses (Linha Verde) leave every 20 minutes for the city centre. The 'Aero-bus' serves the main hotels. Oporto's Pedras Rubras Airport is 15km (9 miles) north of the city centre, and Faro Airport is 7km (4 miles) from the centre of town; there are buses to Faro and other resorts on the Algarve.

Taxis can also take you to the city centre. All have meters, and lists of charges for out-of-town journeys. In Lisbon, taxi drivers are entitled to charge an excess for luggage over 30kg (66lb).

The national carrier

By rail

Nowhere in Portugal is yet linked to the superfast TGV system, but there's a busy international (and national) train service. A daily train makes the Paris–Lisbon run. An Autorail service operates between Paris and Lisbon via Oporto all the year round. Madrid–Lisbon (usually twice a day) takes around 10 hours.

There are routes from northern Spain (Galicia) and southern Spain (Seville) into Portugal. These tend to be slow and time-consuming. Once *in* Portugal, you have a good fast north–south route (Oporto–Lisbon–Faro) as well as slow, scenic rides, if you care for them, especially in the north. But on some of these routes trains have been replaced by bus services.

Choose your transport

By road

Good roads link Portugal with its neighbour Spain at numerous border points. Main east–west routes to Lisbon are from Seville via Beja; from Badajos via Elvas; from Salamanca via Vilar Formoso. The main border crossing in the north is at Valença do Minho. Journey time is two days from most of Europe. Driving from England, using the Channel ferries or the Channel Tunnel, allow three days; or, via Plymouth–Santander or Portsmouth–Bilbao, two. There are drivers who boast of doing the journey faster, but don't try. Road accident figures are appallingly high.

Getting Around

By car

Motorists, whether using either their own car or a hire car, should take note of two important warnings. First, many roads are in poor condition and have poor visibility. A drive of 200km (125 miles) is probably enough for one day. Second, Portuguese drivers are unpredictable. Portugal has the worst record for road accidents in Europe.

Parking on the praça

Oporto station

Speed limits are as follows: 60kmph (37mph) in built-up areas, 120kmph (74mph) on motorways, 100kmph (62mph) on main roads and 90kmph (56mph) on country roads. Good progress can be made on the following stretches of road: the motorway between Setúbal, Lisbon, Oporto and Braga; the main highway from Vilar Formoso on the Spanish border to the junction with the motorway at Albergaria; and from Setúbal to the Algarve between Grândola and Albufeira. A new stretch of road between Porto, Vila Real and Bragança is under construction.

The driver of a hire car must be at least 21 years old and have possessed a driving licence for a full year.

By rail

Modern express trains operate between Lisbon and Oporto. On other lines, most trains stop fairly frequently. Journeys on the rural lines, particularly in the north, can be quite unforgettable experiences, e.g. the coastal line from Viana do Castelo to Caminha, on the Douro line from Oporto to Pêso da Régua and on the Tua line as far as Mirandela. Tickets must always be bought in advance. For travellers intending to make full use of the rail network, a tourist ticket (*bilhete turistico*) for either 7, 14 or 21 days is worth enquiring about.

There are four train stations in Lisbon: Estacão Santa Apolónia for express trains to the north and east (Coimbra/Oporto, Guarda, Marvão, Elvas and Spain); Estacão Cais do Sodré for outlying suburbs east of Cascais and Estoril (via Belém); Estacão Rossío for Sintra and Figueira da Foz; Estacão Barreiro (south of the Tagus) for the south and southeast (Algarve, Beja, Evora).

There are three railway stations in Oporto: São Bento for local train services; Campanhã for international services to Lisbon, Spain and Douro Valley; and Trindade for the narrow-gauge service to Guimarães and Póvoa da Varzim.

By bus

The bus network is comprehensive, with regular services linking most towns and villages. The biggest bus company is the state-owned Rodoviária Nacional (RN). Express coaches (*expressos*) operate on the popular routes.

Facts for the Visitor

Travel documents

Citizens of Great Britain, Australians, Americans and Canadians need nothing more than a valid passport for a three-month stay.

All non-EU visitors must show a valid passport to enter Portugal. On arrival, your passport will be stamped with a 60-day tourist visa. No one with a tourist visa is permitted to work in Portugal.

Tourist information

In the UK: The address of the Portuguese National Tourist Office is New Bond Street House, 1–5 New Bond Street, London W1Y ONP, tel: 0171-493 3873.

In the US: Portuguese National Tourist Office, 590 Fifth Avenue, New York, NY 10036-4704, tel: 212-354 4403.

In Portugal:The headquarters is Direcção Geral do Turismo, Avenida António Augusto de Águiar, 1000 Lisbon. All the places on the tourist routes have a *turismo* (tourist information office) where staff will help with finding accommodation:

Aveiro: Rua João Mendonça 8, tel: (034) 23680, fax: (034) 28326.
Braga: Avenida Central 1, tel: (053) 22550, fax: (053) 613660.
Coimbra: Largo da Portagem, tel: (039) 23886, fax: (039) 25576.
Évora: Praça de Geraldo, tel: (066) 22671.
Faro: Rua da Misericórdia 8–12, tel: (089) 803667, fax: (089) 803673.
Lisbon: Praça dos Restauradores, tel: (01) 3463314 or 346 3624.
Oporto: Rua Clube Dosfenianos 25, tel: (02) 323303, fax: (02) 2084548.
Sebútal: Praça de Quebedo, tel: (065) 29507.

Currency and exchange

The *escudo*, which is divided into 100 *centavos*, is the basic unit of currency. The smallest coin is the 1 *escudo* piece; the largest is the 200 *escudo* coin. 1,000 *escudos* is called a *conto*. Notes go from 500 to 10,000 *escudos*. The symbol for the *escudo* is the same as for the dollar sign, but is written after the number of *escudos* (and before the number of *centavos*). Thus, 75$oo is 75 *escudos*; 75$5o is 75 *escudos* and 50 *centavos*.

Outside normal banking hours, there are currency exchanges at Lisbon's Santa Apolónia railway station as well

Check the exchange rate first

as at the airports. Traveller's cheques, which can be exchanged at all banks, entail paying a commission, but the rate is higher than for cash. You will also find numerous cashpoints in the cities and large towns. All major credit cards are accepted in the more expensive hotels, restaurants and shops.

Tipping
A service charge is included in the menu prices at restaurants but a small tip is always appreciated by waiters and customary if the service has been good. Hairdressers, hotel staff and taxi drivers also expect to be tipped.

Opening times
Banks: Monday to Friday, 8.30–11.45am, 1–2.30pm. Many banks, especially those in cities and tourist resorts, stay open during the lunch break.

Shops: There is no law governing shop opening times in Portugal, but shops are usually open Monday to Friday, 9am–1pm and 3–7pm, Saturday, 9am–1pm. Supermarkets often stay open during the lunch break. Shops in the new shopping centres frequently open at 10am but do not close until 10pm or later.

Museums: Most museums are closed on Monday with the exception of the Sintra, Mafra and Queluz castles near Lisbon, which are closed on Tuesday or Wednesday. Museum opening times can often change at short notice.

Post Offices: Monday to Friday, 9am–1pm, 3–6pm. Closed Saturday and Sunday.

Festival of São João

Public holidays
There are four national holidays: 25 April (National Day), 10 June (Camões Day), 5 October (Republic Day) and 1 December (Independence Day).

Other holidays are 1 January, Good Friday, 1 May, Corpus Christi, 15 August (Feast of the Assumption), 1 November (All Saints' Day), 8 December (Feast of the Immaculate Conception) and 25 December.

There are also local festivals such as 13 June in Lisbon and 24 June in Oporto (São João). There is only one day's public holiday at Easter, Whitsuntide and Christmas.

Active holidays
Portugal has some fine golf courses on the Algarve and near Lisbon. The nature reserves in the mountain regions provide plenty of opportunities for keen walkers, while the rivers in the north are very popular with anglers and canoeists. The *Turismo de Habitacão* often supply information on sporting facilities such as tennis, riding, fishing and hunting. Suggestions are included in the Places section of this guide.

Postal services
Cafés and kiosks with a CTT sign sell stamps (*selos*) and have public telephones. Be certain to write *Via Aerea* on all airmail items.

Telephone
To make international calls, look for phone boxes marked 'Credifone', which take phone cards, available from post offices and stationery shops. You can also make calls – international and local – from the post offices. In Lisbon there is also a phone office in the Rossío, open every day from 9am–11pm; in Oporto, there is one in Praça da Liberdade (same hours). Cheap rate phone calls start at 6pm.

To call direct to the UK, dial 0044, plus the area code and phone number. For the US and Canada, dial 097 1 plus the full phone number. AT&T, tel: 05017–1288; MCI, tel: 05017–1234; Sprint, tel: 05017–1877.

Calls are cheaper after 6pm

Time
Portugal uses Central European Time, i.e. one hour ahead of GMT in winter, but two hours ahead in summer (end of March to end of September).

Medical
Visitors are strongly advised to ensure that they have adequate holiday insurance. British citizens are entitled to receive medical care from the Portuguese health service. A high proportion of the costs will be met by the authorities but visitors must have an E111 form, which is obtainable from post offices.

Chemists (*farmácias*) are open Monday to Friday, 9am–1pm, 3–7pm, Saturday 9am–1pm. Chemists in urban areas operate a night and Sunday rota.

Emergencies
Tel: 115 for police and ambulance.

Theft
Visitors to tourist areas such as the Algarve and Lisbon need to be on their guard at all times against opportunist thefts. Always lock any valuables away in the boot of the car. Stolen documents are often discarded by thieves and may be handed in at police stations.

Diplomatic Representation
Great Britain: Rua São Domingos 37, Lisbon, tel: (01) 3961191; Avenida Boavista 3072, 4100 Oporto, tel: (02) 6184789.
United States: Avenida Forças Armadas, Lisbon, tel: (01) 7266600; Rua Júlio Dinis 826–3º, 4000 Oporto, tel: (02) 6063094.

Accommodation

Pousada at Guimarães

Portugal offers accommodation to suit every taste and every purse. There are many top-class hotels in Lisbon and by the coast in the main tourist regions. They are classified officially with stars: one star is basic accommodation, five stars is luxury. Children up to the age of six who sleep in the same room as their parents are usually free and children from seven to 12 pay half tariff. In the tourist areas by the coast there are many holiday apartments, also given categories according to specified criteria.

Albergaria are good quality pensions. An *estalagem* is a hotel furnished to a high standard, often in a rural location. A basic pension is called a *pensão* (with board) or a *residencial* (breakfast only). Independent travellers often prefer the *pousadas* (usually in the middle to high price range). They are located in attractive settings or near places of historical interest. They make good bases from which to explore the surrounding area. These *pousadas* are often housed in old castles or monasteries and have a limited number of beds available. Stays are restricted to a maximum of three nights and reservation is essential. The Portuguese National Tourist Office (*see page 97*) are able to supply a full list of *pousadas*. In Portugal contact Enatur, Pousadas de Portugal, Avenida Santa Joana a Princesa 10, 1700 Lisboa, tel: (01) 848 1221, fax: 805846 or 848 4349.

In recent years an organisation known as **Turismo de Habitaçao** (TH) has become well established, particularly in northern Portugal. The type of accommodation offered is, like the *pousadas*, in older premises, often of historic interest, such as *palácios* in towns or *quintas* in rural settings. A minimum stay is three nights. **Turismo Rural** (TR) is a similar organisation offering simpler accommodation, and **Agroturismo** (AT) provides rooms in country farmhouses. Contact PRIVETUR, Travessa de Cima dos Quartéis 24-2A, 1200 Lisbon, tel: (01) 691508 or 741672, fax: (058) 711444 for northern Portugal. The local *turismo* offices will also supply information on availability of accommodation in the area.

Youths on parade

Camp sites

There are about 100 camp sites by the coast and in the larger towns. Most of these are well looked after, particularly those run by **Orbitur**. For a full list of addresses contact the Portuguese National Tourist Office (*see page 97*). Book shops sell a guide entitled **Roteira Campista**.

Youth hostels

With a total of only 18 youth hostels in the country reservation is essential, especially for July and August.

Hotel selection

The following suggestions from the most popular centres are listed according to three categories: $$$ = expensive; $$ = moderate; $ = cheap

Characteristic comfort

Albufeira
$$$Montechoro, 3.3km (2 miles) to the north, tel: 859423, fax: 859947. First-class location. **$$Auramar**, Praia dos Aveiros, tel: 513337, fax: 513327. Friendly family apartments close to the town centre.

Aljubarrota
$$Casa da Padeira, tel: (0642) 48272. A nice hotel (TH).

Amarante
$$Navarras, Rua António Carneiro, tel: (055) 424036, fax: 425891. Modern hotel in a central location with pool.

Aveiro
$$Alfonso V, Rua Dr Manuel das Neves 65, tel: (034) 25191, fax: 381111. Aveiro's top hotel.

Beja
The exclusive **$$$***pousada* in the São Francisco monastery has only recently opened.

Braga
The best – but not the cheapest – accommodation is to be found near the Jesús do Monte hill: **$$$Do Parque** and **$$$Elevador** (TH). **$$Casa dos Lagos** (TH).

Cascais
$$$Estalagem do Farol. Nostalgic villa in an isolated position on the edge of town by the sea. **$$Casa da Pérgola**, Avenida Valbom 13. Enchanting, 'old Portuguese' hotel in the town centre (TH).

Coimbra
$$$Tivoli Coimbra, Rua João Machado 4, tel: (039) 33340. Opened in 1990, it's the best hotel in town. **$$Residencial Alentejana**, Rua Dr Henriques Seco 1, tel: (039) 25924. Old villa near the Praça da República. **$Residencial Antunes**, Rua Castro Matoso 8, tel: (039) 23048. Peaceful spot by the aqueduct.

The pousada at Évora

Estremoz
$$$Rainha Santa Isabel. A luxurious palace *pousada*.

Évora
$$$Pousada dos Lóios, Largo Conde de Flor, tel: (066) 24051, fax: 27248. Said to be the finest *pousada* in Por-

Guimarães sea view

tugal. **$$Riviera**, Rua 5 de Outubro 49, tel: (066) 23304, fax: 20467. Quiet spot with local colour.

Faro

$$$Eva, Avenida da República 1, tel: 803354, fax: 802304. View of harbour. Rooftop swimming pool. **$Casa de Lumena**, Praça A. Herculano 27, tel: 801990. Older premises near town centre.

Guimarães

$$$Casa de Sezim, famous for the fine *vinho verde* produced here. 4km (2½ miles). TH offer other fine hotels in the region. **Paço de São Cipriano**, 6km (4 miles). For further information, ask at the *turismo*.

Guincho

$$$Hotel do Guincho. Luxury hotel in an old fortress.

Lagos

$$$Casa de São Gonçalo, Rua Cândido dos Reis 73, tel: (082) 762171. Quiet 18th-century villa in the town centre. **$Pensão Mar Azul**, Rua 25 de Abril 13, tel: (082) 769749. Basic hotel in the town centre.

Lamego

$$Vila Hostilina (TH). A *quinta* with a panoramic view of Lamego. 1km (½ mile) from the town centre.

Lisbon

Most of the hotels offering accommodation of international standard are to be found in the area around the Pombal Rotunda. **$$$Avenida Palace**, Rua 1 Decembro 123, tel: 346 0151, fax: 342 2884. Luxury hotel near Rossío station. Turn of the century building. **$$$Lapa**, Rua Pau da Bandeira 4, tel: 395 0005, fax: 395 0665. The best of the best. In the diplomatic quarter, with swimming pool. **$$Janelas Verdes**, Rua Janelas Verdes 47, tel: 396 8143, fax: 396 8144. New, tastefully appointed, historical setting. **$$Nacional**, Rua Castilho 34, tel: 355 4433, fax: 356 1122. New hotel in good position with garage. **$Borges**, Rua Garrett 108, tel: 346 1951, fax: 867896. Old hotel in the centre of Chiado. Quiet spot. **$Casa de São Mamede**, Rua da Escola Politécnica 159, tel: 396 3166. Friendly pension in delightful premises.

Youth hostels: Rua Andrade Corvo 46, not in city centre but easily reached by train to Cascais; **Catalazete**, Estrada Marginal, Oeiras.

Luso

$$Vila Duparchy on a hill overlooking the town, tel: (039) 93120.

Marvão
$$Pousada Santa Maria on the edge of the town, tel: (045) 93201, fax: 93440.

Marvão

Oporto
$$$Infante de Sagres, Praça D. Filipa de Lencastre 62, tel: (02) 200 8101, fax: 31493. Well-managed luxury hotel in the traditional style. In the city centre. **$$$Le Méridien Porto**, Avenida da Boavista 1466, tel: (02) 600 1913, fax: 600 2031. Smart business hotel with restaurant on terrace. **$$São João**, Rua do Bonjardim 120, tel: (02) 200 1662, fax: 316114. Family hotel but with something extra, in the city centre. **$$Internacional**, Rua do Almada 131, tel: (02) 200 5032. Restored turn-of-the-century building.The cheaper pensions are to be found in the poorer area around the São Bento station.

Santiago do Cacém
$$$Pousada de São Tiago, tel: (069) 22459, fax: 22459. **$$Quinta da Ortiga**, tel: (069) 22871, fax: 22073. 3km (2 miles) from the town centre.

Serpa
$$$Pousada de São Gens on a hill overlooking Serpa.

Setúbal
$$$Pousada de São Filipe. In Setúbal castle. Magnificent sea views.

Sintra
$$Pensão Sintra, recently renovated villa with a garden and a swimming pool. The *turismo* can arrange delightful accommodation in private *quintas* (TH).

Sintra

Tomar
The best accommodation is to be found away from the town: **$$Quinta da Anunciada Velha** (TH) in Cem Soldos 3km (2 miles) away, tel: (049) 545218. **$$Pousada S. Pedro** near the Castelo de Bode reservoir (watersports), 12km (7 miles), tel: (049) 3811 5975.

Viana do Castelo
The **$$Vinho-Verde-Quinta Paço d'Anha** (AT) 3km (2 miles) from the town offers comfortable accommodation in beautiful surroundings.

Viseu
$$$Grão Vasco, Rua Gaspar Barreiros, tel: (032) 423432, fax: 427047. The town's main hotel, set in parkland. **$$Maná**, N16, Via Caçador, tel: (032) 479243, fax: 478744. On the edge of town, good restaurant.

Index

Albergaria 59
Albufeira 46
Alcácer do Sal 43
Alcobaça 37
Alentejo 41–2
Alfama, Lisbon 20–3
Aljubarrota 39
Alter de Chao 50
Alveiro 58
Amarante 78
Armaçâo de Pêra 46
Avenida da Liberdade, Lisbon 23

Bairro Alto, Lisbon 24–5
Baixa, Lisbon 18–20
Basto wine region 81
Batalha 39
Belém 27–9
Braga 73–4
Bragança 80
Buçaco Forest 59

Cabo da Roca 32
Cabo de Sâo Vicente 44
Cabo Espichel 42
Caldas da Rainha 36
Caldas das Taipas 72
Caldas de Monchique 45
Caldas do Gerês 77
Caramulo 60
Carvoeira 46
Casa Museu Guerra Junquiero, Oporto 67
Cascais 30
Castelo de Vide 51
Castelo dos Mouros, Sintra 34
Castro de Avelã 81
Chaves 81
Chiado, Lisbon 24–5
Citânia de Briteiros 72
Clube Nacional de Montanhismo 62
Coimbra 52–7
Conimbriga 57
Convent of the Knights of Christ, Tomar 39
Convento de Jesus, Aveiro 59
Costa da Caparica 42
Costa do Sol 30
Costa Verde 74

Domus Municipalis, Bragança 80
Douro River 78–80
Douro Valley 78–80

Elvas 50
Encontramento 40
Episcopal Palace, Oporto 67
Eposende 75
Estói 46
Estoril 30, 31–2
Estrêla, Lisbon 26
Estremoz 50
Évora 48–9

Faro 46
Fátima 38
Fonseca wine cellars 42

Grândola 43
Guarda 62
Guimaraes 71–2
Guincho 32

Igreja da Misériocordia, Vieu 61
Igreja de Jesus 43
Igreja dos Grilos 67
Ilha de Tavira 47

Jardim Botánico, Coimbra 56

Lagoa Comprida 62
Lagos 44
Lamego 79
Lapa, Lisbon 26
Lima River 77
Lisbon 14–29
Lorvão monastery 60

Mafra 35
Mangualde 61
Manta Rota 47
Manteigas 62
Marvão 51
Mateus 79
Meira Praia (beach) 44
Melgaço 76
Mercado do Bolhão 69
Mertola 47–8
Milreu 46
Minho River 76
Mira de Aire caves 39
Miranda do Douro 80
Miróbriga 44
Misericórdia Church, Oporto 69
Monserrate 34
Monte de Santa Luzia 75
Monte Gordo 47
Mosteiro de Santa Cruz, Coimbra 55
Mosteiro dos Jerónimos 27
Moura 48
Museu Calouste 29
Museu de Arte Moderna, Oporto 69
Museu de Arte Sacra 49
Museu de Automóvel 60
Museu do Azulejo 29
Museu Grão Vasco 61
Museu Machado de Castro, Coimbra 55
Museu Nacional de Arte Artiga, Lisbon 26
Museu Nacional Soares dos Reis, Oporto 70
Museu Regional, Alentejo 44
Museu Regional, Évora 49

Nazaré 37
Nossa Senhora dos Remédios 79

Óbidos 36–7
Ofir 74
Old University, Coimbra 54
Olhão 46–7
Oporto 63–70
Outeiro Seco 81

Paço Real, Sintra 33
Palácio da Pena 34
Palácio dos Condes de Anadia 61
Palácio dos Marquesas da Fronteira 29
Patio da Inquisiçao 56
Penacova 60
Peneda-Geres National Park 76
Peninha 32–3
Pinhão wine region 79
Poço do Inferno 62
Ponte de Barca 77
Ponte de Lima 77
Ponte de Priedade 44
Ponte Maria Pia, Oporto 66
Porto Sandeman lodge 68
Praia da Falésia 46
Praia Dona Ana 44

Queluz 35
Quinta da Bacalhoa 43
Quinta das Lagrimas 57
Quinta das Torres 42–3
Quinta do Lago 46

Reguengos de Monsaraz 48
Ria Formosa 46
Ribatejo 50–1
Rio Sado Delta 43
Rossío 51
Rossío, Lisbon 18
Rotunda, Tomar 40

Sabroso 79
Sagres 44
Santa Comba Dão 60
Santa Margarida da Serra 43
Santa Maria da Vitória monastery 39
Santiago do Cacém 43–4
São Bartolomeu do Mar 75
São Martinho do Porto 37
Sapal de Castro Marim 47
Sé Velha, Coimbra 54
Serpa 48
Serra da Arrabida 42
Serra da Estrêla 61
Serra da Sintra 33
Serra de Alvao 81
Serra de Caramulo 60
Serra de Monchique 45
Serra de Sao Mamede 50
Setúbal 43
Silves 45
Sines 44
Sintra 33–4

Tavira 47
Tomar 39
Torre de Clérigos 70
Torre de Menagem 80

Vale do Lobo 46
Valença do Minho 76
Viana do Castelo 75
Vidago 81
Vila Franca de Xira 51
Vila Nova da Cerveira 76
Vila Praia de Ancora 76
Vila Real 81
Vila Viçosa 50
Vilamoura 46
Viseu 59, 61
Vista Alegre 59